Native Americans Before 1492

The Moundbuilding Centers of the Eastern Woodlands

Kevin Reilly, Series Editor

THE ALCHEMY OF HAPPINESS
Abu Hamid Muhammad al-Ghazzali
translated by Claud Field
Revised and annotated by Elton L. Daniel

LIFELINES FROM OUR PAST
A New World History
L. S. Stavrianos

NATIVE AMERICANS BEFORE 1492
The Moundbuilding Centers of the Eastern Woodlands
Lynda Norene Shaffer

BALKAN WORLDS
The First and Last Europe
Traian Stoianovich

Sources
and
Studies
in World
History

Native Americans Before 1492

The Moundbuilding Centers of the Eastern Woodlands

Lynda Norene Shaffer

M.E. Sharpe
ARMONK, NEW YORK
LONDON, ENGLAND

Copyright © 1992 by M. E. Sharpe, Inc.
80 Business Park Drive, Armonk, New York 10504

Library of Congress Cataloging-in-Publication Data

Shaffer, Lynda, 1944–
Native Americans before 1492 : the moundbuilding centers of the eastern woodlands / Lynda Norene Shaffer.
p. cm. — (Sources and studies in world history)
Includes bibliographical references and index.
ISBN 1-56324-029-7 (C). — ISBN 1-56324-030-0 (P)
1. Mound-builders—East (U.S.) 2. Mississippian culture—East (U.S.)
3. East (U.S.)—Antiquities. I. Title. II. Series.
E78.E2S46 1992
974′.01—dc20
92-28230
CIP

Printed in the United States of America
The paper used in this publication meets the minimum
requirements of American National Standard for
Information Sciences—Permanence of Paper for
Printed Library Materials, ANSI Z 39.48-1984.

∞

(c) BB   10   9   8   7   6   5   4   3   2
(p) BB   10   9   8   7   6   5   4   3   2

To Aunt Frankye and co-explorers of the Missouri Woodlands Lowel and Leslie, and in memory of another who was in our party and still is always on our minds, Emma Jean Jundy Bland White (1942–1979).

To Mother, in memory of Grandmother Lillie Bell Goodman Cox Cook Tomlin MacWilliams (1888–1979) and Great-Grandmother Alice Virginia Carl Goodman (1869–1954), and to all who tell the stories of those who came before.

OLD STUDENTS OF THE NEW PHYSICS

A bulldozer slashed the breast
of the Indian mound—
    back and forth
    back and forth
scraping ancient soil
bone/pottery/prayer
into a dump truck
until the land was flat

      except

for one hip bone.
It stood upright—
a periscope from Mother Earth—
and drew into its dark socket
    the wide-open wound
    with its ragged edge of grass,
    trees standing nearby
    drooped in dust and shock,
    machines receding . . .

A monarch butterfly
drifted over the site.
She lit on the bone,
slowly flexed her wings.
"When I move my wings
energies change around the world
    round and round and
    up . . . up . . . up . . .
    into the sky.
I can cause storm/hurricane/tornado
when I move my wings."

"I know," said the bone.
"Now men have moved me."

          —Marilou Awiakta

CONTENTS

MAPS AND OTHER ILLUSTRATIONS

Illustrations (following page 50)

FOREWORD

I am proud to include Lynda Shaffer's *Native Americans Before 1492: The Moundbuilding Centers of the Eastern Woodlands* in the series "Sources and Studies in World History" not only because it is an interesting history of an important but neglected subject but also because it shows the advantage of taking a global approach. In the hands of a brilliant world historian like Professor Shaffer, we see the region of North America afresh, as part of a rich comparative tapestry. With her as guide, our understanding is shaped by a global vision, a sense of major historical processes, and questions of cultural character that are often beyond the peripheral vision of regional specialists.

This book will be of interest to teachers and students of both Amercian history and world history. Professor Shaffer reminds those who begin the story of American history with European colonization that there was both an earlier and a contemporaneous history of indigenous peoples that strongly affected European experience. English settlement, for instance, was possible north of Florida because the Spanish incursions into this area were repeatedly defeated during the sixteenth century. Further, the patterns of European settlement and the subsequent growth of towns almost exactly duplicated the patterns of Native American settlements and trading centers. We have in this book a formative stage of American history.

World historians too can gain much from this book. When we include American history at all in our surveys of world history, we almost always limit ourselves to the history of Aztec, Maya, and Inca civilizations, ignoring the peoples of what is today the United States. This is so odd (since so many world historians live in North America) that it suggests the continuation of a colonial settler's inability to see the people for the trees. In fact, Europeans cut down both the people and the trees, leveled the earthenwork ceremonial mounds that had testified to Native American cultural creativity and societal complexity, and called their desecrated graveyard a virgin land. This book helps us retrieve that buried past so that we might begin to understand more about not only the people who lived here (and by comparison their contemporaries elsewhere in the world) but also those who conquered and survived.

The "Sources and Studies in World History" series plans to publish other works by Professor Shaffer on regions in Africa and Asia. Together with the present volume, these will in effect constitute a series within the series, exploring several pivotal but poorly understood subjects in world history.

Kevin Reilly

PREFACE

Perhaps I should begin by explaining why a historian of modern China is writing about Eastern North America before 1492. Almost twenty years ago I became convinced that some of the most interesting questions about China could not be answered merely by studying Chinese history, since answering them required an awareness of events outside China as well as comparisons between China and other parts of the world. Thus I became interested in world history. More than ten years ago one of my colleagues, a senior member of the History Department at Tufts University, suggested that the department should offer some sort of world history course that could serve as an introduction to the numerous courses that we offer on Africa, Asia, and Latin America. Those of us who teach these courses (all of whom were then junior) considered the matter and began examining various world history course designs and texts. Often we were dismayed by what we found. Our own areas of expertise were not always well presented, and sometimes they were ignored completely. We thus decided not to use the existing conceptualizations and together set out to reconstruct world history.

As regional specialists we came from a wide variety of historiographical traditions, and there was little agreement among us with regard to themes or theories of history. It thus seemed wise to abandon any preconceived notions of what would be revealed by a global approach to world history. We began, instead, by negotiating a periodization that all could live with, presuming that the aggregation of our individual expertise about each of the globe's regions during each time frame would provide a vision of the whole. What became clear, however, was that we did not have all the pieces. No one on the faculty at that time knew anything about North America north of the Rio Grande prior to 1492. And there were other parts of the world where the accessible literature did not discuss the topics and material that we needed. Confronted by the prospect of working on a puzzle that was missing some of its pieces, I decided to fill these gaps, and thus strayed into what was for me terra incognita.

This journey into the unknown has been full of surprises. The first was the realization that the largest gaps in the literature were not in obscure or insignificant places. One was West Africa, whence came the gold that tempted the Arabs to cross the shifting sands of the Sahara and then lured the Portuguese down the western coast of Africa through unknown seas, thereby changing the fate of the world. Another was in Maritime Southeast Asia, whence came the fine spices that had drawn Indians, Persians, Arabs, Chinese, and finally the Europeans to the straits region and the islands that are now Indonesia. Indeed, had it not been for this lure to the East Indies, Columbus would not have found what we now call the West Indies, nor would the Portuguese have sought a way around Africa to the markets of India. And the greatest gap of all in our knowledge of the world was the most familiar place, in the very heartland of what is now the United States: the moundbuilding region of Eastern North America.

It is my contention that these places were a significant part of one or the other of the two hemisphere-wide arenas that characterized world history prior to the Columbian voyages, and that we therefore need to include them in our vision of world history. I hope to demonstrate this in three separate essays, each of which will present the history of a region in a way that is consistent with the interpretations of specialists and, at the same time, in a way that can be used by scholars and teachers of world history. This essay on Eastern North America is the first, and it will be followed shortly by those on Maritime Southeast Asia and West Africa.

It is also my contention that a knowledge of the traditional institutions and patterns of interaction within these regions is critical to an understanding of the dynamics of world history. When I set out to write about them I was not looking for similarities and had no intention of comparing them with each other or with other places. Yet in the course of studying the relevant literature, I began to discern not only differences but also certain similarities in their histories, social structures, and political institutions. I also realized that it was precisely the features that they had in common that made these regions seem so different from much of the rest of the world, especially from those places upon which world historians usually focus their attention. In fact, it may well be that the reason that most world historians have overlooked their significance is that their political and economic dynamics have been poorly understood. Thus I plan a fourth essay that will take a comparative approach to the histories of these three regions. It will provide an analysis of their traditional institutions and patterns of interaction as well as an assessment of the role that they have played in world history.

Since 1992 is the quincentennial anniversary of the first Columbian voyage, the decision to make this study of Eastern North America before 1492 the first of these essays to be published was not a difficult one. One hundred years ago, in 1892, there were many enthusiastic celebrations of the anniversary, but that has not been the case this year. There has been a discernible reluctance to celebrate in 1992. In some ways this reluctance is a mark of progress, since it is the result of an increased awareness that Columbus's arrival was followed by much suffering, especially on the part of those who were already here and by those who were brought here in bondage from Africa. Given this awareness, some have argued that there is nothing to celebrate, and others have refrained from celebrating since they are unwilling to have the spirit of their festivities dampened by any references to the tragedies that followed.

There is, however, a way out of this impasse, a way that was discovered many decades ago by the people of Mexico. First and foremost they celebrate themselves, their very existence, as a people of multiple ancestries and Mestizo culture. They do not consider themselves to be the descendants of one side or the other, but the result of the personal and cultural encounters that began when Columbus came. And they have pointed out the obvious, that it is possible to celebrate one's own birthdays without endorsing everything that one's parents and other progenitors have ever done to each other or to anyone else. It is precisely because the Mexicans have learned to acknowledge and celebrate their complicated and multiple origins that they are able to celebrate unabashedly the beginning of the encounters that gave birth to the peoples and cultures of their nation.

We need to try this approach north of the Rio Grande. But in order to do so, we will have to recognize that we are also the result of a long-standing encounter between Native Americans and peoples from other parts of the globe. No doubt it sometimes seems that the history of the encounter was little more than a series of collisions, and that the entanglements that produced us were more often than not the result of close combat. Nevertheless, for better or for worse, here we all are.

To know truly who we are and to be at peace with that knowledge, we must be willing to claim all of our national ancestors, winners of the day and losers too, and we must claim all of our siblings and cousins. We must know their names and their relationships to us. Then we can celebrate the existence of all of us now within the bounds of the United States, and especially the survival of those nations who were here when Columbus sailed.

This need to know applies especially to those whose ancestors lived in the eastern part of what is now the United States. It is their histories and the histories of their interactions with the peoples of the British colonies and of the newly independent American states after 1776 that would create the most intellectual dissonance for most Americans and American historians, were they known to us. The peoples of Eastern North America were and are located upon the stage where the early history of this nation was enacted, and they, too, had a part in the drama. Thus to know their history, before and after 1492, and to consider it to be a part of our own would require a complete reconstruction of our understanding of the very foundations of our nation. No doubt, it is for this reason that it has always been easier to forget those who lived in the Eastern Woodlands and to romanticize those who lived in the West. Even now, when well-intentioned organizers decide to include some Native American group in a quincentennial event, they seem to display an inordinate preference for those peoples living in close proximity to the Pacific or at least well west of the Mississippi River.

Fortunately, the inclusion of Eastern North America within world history does not present such fundamental problems. Quite the contrary, it fits neatly into the larger picture. With regard to the years before 1500, which are the subject of this essay, Eastern North America provides a wealth of new material about topics and themes that are already the concerns of world historians. The story describes a process of human adaptation to a unique physical environment and provides an illuminating example of localization that involved the domestication of many plants but no animals, except for the dog. It adds to our knowledge of how rivers have served as the focus of civilizations. And it offers an even broader comparative framework for an analysis of the emergence of interaction spheres and exchange networks as well as the emergence of towns and central places marked by monumental architecture. A knowledge of Eastern North America before 1492 also helps to explain why the peoples of the moundbuilding region were able to defeat the Spanish, and why, if we leave them out, our vision of the world will be incomplete.

Once I began writing about the moundbuilding region, I realized that it was terra incognita only in a professional sense. In fact, by the time that I was thirteen years old, I was intimately acquainted with some seven locales within its bounds. My first home, and the one to which I always returned throughout an itinerant childhood, was my maternal grandmother's farm, near the banks of the Neches River in Cherokee County, Texas. It is almost within shouting distance of the mounds at the Davis Site. My father was born on a sheep ranch next to the Marais des Cygnes, a tributary of the Osage River. He became a liaison pilot in the U.S. Army, and thus sandwiched between the years that the family lived in Japan and Germany, we enjoyed a veritable tour of the moundbuilding region, with postings in Wisconsin, Illinois, Kansas, Oklahoma, and Alabama. And when we were between stations, I lived with paternal cousins on a farm in northern Missouri, only a few miles from Fort Osage, on the Missouri River. I now find it utterly amazing that I had never heard of an Indian mound, much less seen one, until I began studying world history.

In all these places I spent much of my time in the woods. I can still conjure up the contours and textures of many a ravine and gully, for I was often drawn to the bottoms, to the silt-laden floors where the creeks run. I do not know why I spent so many hours in the woods, unless it was a habit acquired from tagging along behind my maternal grandmother and great grandmother as they went about their various tasks. Thus in many ways, visiting the mounds and writing about the peoples who built them have been for me a long-awaited journey home.

It is, of course, unwise to do what I have done, to be an interloper in someone else's field of specialization. The hazards are many, and the only reason that I have survived to tell about it, so far, is that those who work in these fields have been generous with their time and expertise. Many have assisted me in this study, and although I cannot name them all, I would like to take this opportunity to thank those friends and colleagues whose help was critical at various stages. It was two historians of colonial America, Dane Morrison and John Brooke, who impressed upon me the importance of the moundbuilding peoples. Susan Lee, a graduate student in archaeology at the University of Arkansas, was responsible for my first trip to Cahokia, and she has been most generous in sharing her materials on Mississippian artifacts with me. Joan Lester, an expert on Native American crafts in New England, head curator of the Boston Children's Museum, and an instructor in the American Studies Program at Tufts, has performed innumerable favors, and her expertise has been significant in shaping my perspective on the material culture. Phyllis Fischer read an early draft of this essay and provided invaluable editorial assistance. Michael Weber and Kevin Reilly have spoken many encouraging words, and without their assistance it might have been a great many years before this manuscript became a book. And I must thank Marilou Awiakta for letting me use one of her poems as the book's epigraph, for encouraging me to get my red cowboy boots, and for reminding me that life is supposed to be fun, at least some of the time.

I am also indebted to all those people in Native American history and archaeology who were willing to assist an unknown intruder who came asking for favors and claiming to be a historian of China and the world. Several people at the University of Massachusetts at Amherst—Dena F. Dincauze, Robert J. Hasenstab, and Michael S. Nassaney—provided me with their manuscripts, both published and unpublished. Kathleen Byrd, State Archaeologist of Louisiana, and Nancy W. Hawkins, also at Louisiana's Division of Archaeology, were always willing to answer questions and discuss problems of interpretation on the telephone, and I was impressed not only by the breadth of their expertise but also by the professional and diplomatic manner in which they approached the controversies in North American archaeology. And I am grateful to Frederick Hoxie, Director of the D'Arcy McNickle Center for the Study of American Indian History at the Newberry Library. His open-minded spirit and generous hospitality made it possible for me to attend conferences and institutes intended for those who study American history.

It is customary at this point in a preface for the author to assume responsibility for any mistakes that might remain in the text and for the interpretations contained therein, and to absolve all of the persons just acknowledged of any responsibility for them. With regard to this essay, the making of such a statement is not a perfunctory exercise. These persons were invaluable in helping me find materials. Some also helped to clarify the issues when I was confronted by mysterious contradictions in the literature. But they had no way of anticipating what I would do with the materials and information that they provided.

There are many controversies in North American archaeology. As a Chinese historian, I do not harbor unrealistic expectations of harmony within ivory towers. Not so very long ago, before and during the McCarthy period, China experts were subjected to a veritable inquisition, and controversies of various kinds, some fruitful and some not, still flourish in the field. Nevertheless, I was taken aback by the nature of some of the disputes in North American archaeology and by the ways in which they are pursued by some of the experts on the Eastern Woodlands. Long before I finished this study, it became clear to me that such controversies would make it exceedingly difficult to write a book about the moundbuilding region that would please all the archaeologists, especially since I did not want to write a book that would be more about their disagreements than about the peoples of this region.

Thus I found that there are some advantages to being an outsider. I was free, for example, to come to my own conclusions, without fear of consequences. In return for this freedom, I have taken seriously my responsibilities and have exercised great care to distinguish well-established facts from, first, data and interpretations based upon good evidence but which are nevertheless disputed and, second, various hypotheses that are essentially educated guesses made by experts in the field. Only on a few occasions have I omitted any reference in the text to the fact that a statement from an authority has been questioned. Such disclaimers were omitted only when I believed that the evidence was overwhelmingly in the favor of the authority followed, and in all such instances the existence of a disagreement *is* indicated in the notes.

Though I have often felt that I was making my way through a field of mines, I was never tempted to turn back. What I was finding was altogether too interesting.

Somerville, Massachusetts
Spring 1992

Native Americans Before 1492

The Moundbuilding Centers of the Eastern Woodlands

1 INTRODUCTION

Only two hundred years ago, in the woodlands of Eastern North America, there were tens of thousands of large earthen mounds, all of which had been built by Native Americans. They were impressive structures. Visitors who saw them were amazed by the size of many, by their number, and by the intricacy of their design.[1] Yet the significance of these earthworks, indeed, their very existence, is one of the best kept secrets of American history. Even the people who now live on or beside the mound sites are more likely to be familiar with the Native American past of Mexico, the Andes, or the U.S. Southwest than with the heritage of their own region.

Before 1492, moundbuilding centers in Eastern North America could be found from the Great Lakes region in the north to the Gulf of Mexico coast in the south, from the eastern portions of the Great Plains to the Appalachian Mountains. They were built over a period of roughly four thousand years. Banana Bayou, one of the earliest earthen mound sites so far discovered, is located on Avery Island in Iberia Parish, on the Louisiana coast, and has been dated tentatively to 2490 B.C.[2] The latest sites date from sometime around A.D. 1700.

Two hundred years ago almost all the mounds were still safely outside the bounds of the English-speaking settler colonies. Until about 1800, these colonies were generally confined to the Atlantic seaboard, east of the Appalachians. Thereafter, the number of mounds was reduced as waves of settlers from the east, continually reinforced by a flood of European immigrants, poured over the Appalachian Mountains and began plowing them down. In the twentieth century the mounds have been assaulted not only by farmers but also by vandals seeking valuable artifacts and highway-builders who have bulldozed their way through many, if not most sites. Nevertheless, a great many mounds still stand.

On occasion, the European-Americans who came upon the mounds and were amazed by them had the wisdom to ask the local Native American peoples about them. In Illinois in 1778, for example, Chief Baptist of the Kaskaskias was approached by a group of American Revolutionary War soldiers led by George Rogers Clark. They asked Chief Baptist about elaborate earthworks that they had seen near the Mississippi. The earthworks, he answered, were the outer fortifications of an old palace. It had belonged to the ancestors of the Native Americans when they had "covered the whole," when they had had large towns and been "as numerous as trees in the woods."[3]

Many of the newcomers, however, were unwilling to believe that Native Americans could have built such imposing structures and felt it necessary to concoct fantastic theories about their origins. In the nineteenth century, various people argued that the mounds had been built by the Lost Tribes of Israel, or the Vikings, or sixteenth-century Spanish explorers. And in the twentieth century, Erich von Daniken's *Chariots of the Gods* has attributed the mounds to creatures from outer space.[4]

But Chief Baptist knew whereof he spoke. Indeed, there had been a time when Native Americans towns and villages did cover many of the river valleys of Eastern North America. Although modern demographers might not agree that people were as numerous as the trees, one can say that the Native Americans numbered in the millions. Although for many years the pre–European contact population of North America north of the Rio Grande was said to be only about two million, recent scholarship indicates that this figure is a gross underestimate. In 1983 Henry F. Dobyns published an estimate of eighteen million, a figure that remains controversial. Nevertheless, the estimates of others do seem to be climbing upward toward this mark. Two important studies came out in 1987, one estimating more than seven million and another estimating a population of about twelve million. The latter, based upon settlement patterns revealed by archaeological explorations, tends to support Dobyns's assumptions and methods, even though its author concludes with a lower estimate.[5]

Both archaeological evidence and explorers' accounts suggest that a large part of this population was concentrated within the moundbuilding region of Eastern North America. These sources also indicate that the mounds marked the centers of political and economic networks. Ceremonial goods and elite burials are concentrated at these sites, and so was military power. Archaeologists refer to the people who ruled from these centers as "paramount chiefs." They were the heads of alliance networks, possibly because of their prestige or control of scarce resources, or because of their superior military might. And through these networks they could command the loyalty and often the tribute of less powerful chiefs and the peoples they led. Paramount chiefs encountered by the Spanish and French were known as "Great Suns," and, just as Chief Baptist suggested, they lived in palaces—in large and elaborately decorated wooden structures—which were built on the top of high platform mounds. Specially designated groups known as "noble allies" and "honored people" also resided at these centers, and so did much larger numbers of "commoners"—farmers whose fields were nearby, hunters, traders, and artisans.

It is also clear from goods found in the graves of elite persons that moundbuilding centers participated in exchange networks that eventually grew to almost continental proportions. Products from far-off places can be found at many sites, but they tend to be concentrated at the largest centers. Some of the more notable items on a long list that appear to have enjoyed wide circulation include Rocky Mountain stones used to make cutting edges, minerals from the upper reaches of the Mississippi used to make paint pigments, marine shells from Florida, copper from the Great Lakes, stone pipes from the Ohio River valley, and mica from southern Appalachia.

The construction of moundbuilding centers can be divided into three separate epochs. During the first epoch, which took place during the Late Archaic Period (ca. 1500–700 B.C.), such activity was confined to the Lower Mississippi River valley and adjacent areas. The largest center, a site that archaeologists call Poverty Point, was a few miles west of the Mississippi River in northeastern Louisiana. A second moundbuilding epoch took place during what is known either as the Woodlands Period or the Adena-Hopewell Period (ca. 500 B.C. to A.D. 400). It was during this epoch, when the most important centers were concentrated in southern Ohio on tributaries that flow south into the Ohio River, that the construction of moundbuilding centers first spread throughout much of the Eastern Woodlands.

A third moundbuilding epoch (ca. A.D. 700–1700), which archaeolo-

CHRONOLOGY OF THE MOUNDBUILDING REGION

Ice Age Hunters and Gatherers   12,0000–8000 B.C.*
Extinction of Ice Age animals (9000 B.C.)

Early Archaic Period   8000–6000 B.C.
Localization, use of atlatl

Middle Archaic Period   6000–3000 B.C.
Sedentary habits emerge

Late Archaic Period   3000–500 B.C.
Population increase, long-distance exchange
Domestication of indigenous plants
Elite burials, copper in use in north
Pottery in some southern locales

First Moundbuilding Epoch (Late Archaic Period)   **1500–700 B.C.**
Poverty Point Cultural Area
Lower Mississippi Valley

Second Moundbuilding Epoch (Woodlands Period)   **500 B.C.–A.D. 400**
Adena-Hopewell Period
  Adena   500–100 B.C.
  Ohio River valley
  Hopewell   200 B.C.–A.D. 400
  Hopewellian sites throughout moundbuilding region
  Regionwide integration of exchange networks
  Pottery and corn found throughout region
  Increased use of indigenous domesticates
  Spread of bow and arrow (A.D. 300–600)

Third Moundbuilding Epoch   **A.D. 700–1731**
The Mississippian Period
  Palisaded towns, hoes, ball courts
  Reliance upon corn, beans, and other crops
  Cahokia   A.D. 700–1250
  Major Spanish invasions   A.D. 1513–1543
  Postcontact survivals   A.D. 1550–1731
  French defeat Natchez   A.D. 1731

---

*Most of the dates in this chronology are approximations. Especially with regard to the Archaic Period, many are based upon limited data and are subject to change as more data are analyzed and new findings reported. Although there is general agreement regarding this chronology, some scholars would use slightly different dates to define the various periods.

gists refer to as the Mississippian, witnessed the rise of Cahokia, a paramount center located on the Mississippi River, near what is now East St. Louis, Illinois. Between A.D. 900 and 1200, it was many times larger than any other center in Eastern North America. After its decline, a number of more modest centers flourished. Some survived the arrival of the Spanish, and at least one, that of the Natchez in what is now western Mississippi, survived into the eighteenth century.

Almost all of the moundbuilding centers were located within the Eastern Woodlands. This temperate, but relatively southern, forested region provided an ecological setting unlike any other in the world. There are no extensive forests in the temperate zone of the Southern Hemisphere, and all but one in the Northern Hemisphere are much further north. (Only the forests on the steep mountainsides of China's Yangzi River drainage share the Eastern Woodlands' southern temperate position.) Florida is at the same latitude as the Sahara Desert, and even Minnesota and Wisconsin, places usually thought of as northern, are, in fact, at the same latitude as Italy.

It should be emphasized, however, that the moundbuilding region was essentially a human creation—the result of cultural continuities that emerged from ceremonial and exchange networks—and that no single feature of the North American landscape, not even the Eastern Woodlands, shares with it exactly the same boundaries. The Woodlands, for example, extend north of the Great Lakes for a considerable distance and east of the Appalachian Mountains all the way to the Atlantic Ocean. But almost all moundbuilding centers were located south of the Great Lakes, and except in the Southeast (in the Carolinas, Georgia, Alabama, and Florida), almost all were located west of the Appalachian Mountains. It was only during the second epoch, when sites in southern Ohio were predominant, that centers could be found within the Lake Ontario drainage, in what is now New York State and the southeastern part of Ontario, Canada. On the other hand, during the third epoch when the largest center was at the mouth of the Missouri River, they extended westward along this river and its tributaries onto the Great Plains, well outside the bounds of the Woodlands.

Perhaps the best way to define the boundaries of the moundbuilding region would be to identify the four riverine drainage basins that it included. (See Map 1.) The largest part of the region was the eastern two-thirds of the Mississippi River drainage, from present-day Nebraska in the west to New York in the east, and from Minnesota in the

Map 1. **The Moundbuilding Region.** The abbreviations MS, MO, AR, OH, and TN identify the Mississippi River and four of its tributaries, the Missouri, Arkansas, Ohio, and Tennessee rivers. The asterisks mark the principal centers of moundbuilding during each of the three epochs: I. Poverty Point (ca. 1500 to 700 B.C.); II. Adena-Hopewell (ca. 500 B.C. to A.D. 400); III. Mississippian (ca. A.D. 700 to 1731).

north to Louisiana in the south. The region's second largest part was the Gulf Coast drainage basin from the Neches River in eastern Texas to the northern edge of the Everglades in Florida. These two basins were by far the largest and most important parts of the region. In addition, it included two adjacent areas. One was the southernmost part of the Atlantic Ocean drainage, from the Pee Dee River in North Carolina to southern Florida, and the other was the Lake Ontario drainage, which included much of New York and a small part of Ontario. (See Maps 2a and 2b.)

Unlike the ocean-linked networks of interaction that developed in Eastern North America after the Europeans came, those before 1492

Maps 2a and 2b. **Parts of the Moundbuilding Region Outside the Mississippi River Drainage.** For the most part, the moundbuilding region was located within the Mississippi River drainage basin. The only parts of the region that lay outside this basin were the Gulf Coast drainage basin from eastern Texas to Florida, the Atlantic drainage from South Carolina to Florida, and some locales within the Great Lakes drainage basin.

Map 2a. **Mound Sites Within the Great Lakes Drainage Basin**

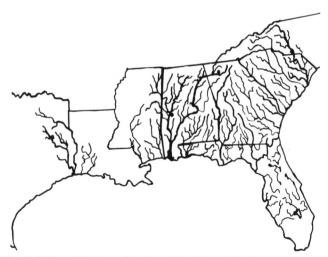

Map 2b. **The Gulf Coast Drainage Basin and the Atlantic Drainage from South Carolina to Florida**

faced inward toward the Mississippi River, and most of the eastern seaboard was a hinterland, on the far side of the Appalachians. West of the Woodlands, the Great Plains formed an ecological barrier, and except along the rivers that flowed into the Mississippi, the peoples there remained distinct from those of the moundbuilding region. Poverty Point in Louisiana, the largest center during the Late Archaic Moundbuilding Epoch, was located within sight of the Mississippi, and so was Cahokia in Illinois, the largest center during the third, Mississippian epoch. And during the second epoch when moundbuilding centers were concentrated in southern Ohio, they were near the Ohio River, a tributary of the Mississippi. Indeed, there is good reason to believe that at least some Native American peoples would have considered the Ohio centers to be near the Mississippi, since peoples in the western portion of present-day New York, for example, thought of the Allegheny, the Ohio, and the Mississippi below the Ohio as a single river.[6]

The Mississippi River truly deserves its Indian name, *Missi* [Great] *Sippi* [River]. In the Western Hemisphere, it is the only major river that flows through a temperate zone. Its total drainage area is close to 1,250,000 square miles, an area equal in size to the country of India. Measured from its most distant headwaters in Montana, it flows for 3,741 miles before reaching the Gulf of Mexico. Thus its length is almost equal to that of the 4,000 mile long Amazon River, which lies near the equator and flows through dense tropical forest.

Eastern North America's moundbuilding region is the only one in the hemisphere where the location of large centers was so closely related to a network of rivers. None of the great civilizations in Mesoamerica and the Andes was so closely identified with a large river basin. They generally had their origins in tropical or subtropical climes where the land rises steeply from coastal lowlands to high mountain plateaus, and much of the terrain is marked by numerous narrow and relatively steep drainage basins. In such locales, climate, growing conditions, and resources vary considerably from one elevation to another, and, in general, the earliest exchange networks and political structures brought about a vertical integration of lowland with highland.

Thus it is only the moundbuilding region of Eastern North America that resembles the pattern of the Eastern Hemisphere, where early civilizations were closely identified with rivers: the Tigris–Euphrates, the Nile, the Indus, and the Yellow River in China. Like the Mississippi, these rivers are located in the temperate latitudes, between 30 and 40 degrees north of the equator. There are, however, significant differences between the locales of these early riverine civilizations of Africa and Asia and Eastern North America's moundbuilding region. One of the most important is that a relatively steady and moderate amount of rain reliably falls over the Eastern Woodlands, whereas the Tigris–Euphrates, the Nile, the Indus, and the Yellow rivers flow for most of their courses through arid lands, in some cases through deserts and in others through what were once grasslands. Most of their water supply comes from the mountains where their headwaters are located, far from the coasts.

The ample rainfall in Eastern North America also accounts for another unique feature of the moundbuilding region. The Mississippi has a truly remarkable network of tributaries arrayed around it. A map of its trunkline and all the waterways that flow into it resembles a huge shrub, densely branched all the way out to the twigs. (See Map 3.) The Eastern Hemisphere rivers famous for the civilizations that grew up along them are not enhanced by any such array of tributaries. Because of the arid conditions over most of their drainage areas, they have few, if any, important tributaries, and most provide only a single trunk-line from the mountains to a distant coast.

The tributaries of the Mississippi are like the spokes of a wheel. The Missouri flows from Montana, from the northern end of the Rocky Mountains and all the way across the Great Plains before it enters the Mississippi. Further south, the Arkansas River links the Mississippi with Colorado. The Red River flows from what is now the New Mexico–Texas border to Arkansas, and down through Louisiana to the Mississippi. From the north the upper reaches of the Mississippi and the Illinois rivers link the Mississippi to Lake Superior and Lake Michigan. From the northeast, the Ohio River and its tributaries flow all the way from western New York and Pennsylvania, and from the southeast, the Tennessee River forms a waterway from western Virginia and the southern Appalachian highlands to the Ohio River, shortly before it enters the Mississippi.

Ample amounts of rain sustain the Woodlands, and its relatively southern position provides a considerably longer frost-free season than is typical of temperate forests. As a result, it is a uniquely hospitable environment for both plants and animals, and before 1492 it provided a

12

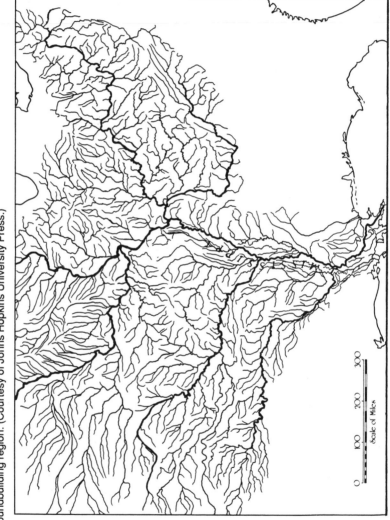

Map 3. **The Hub of the Mississippi River Drainage.** Canoe traffic on this riverine network, as well as several important overland trails that traversed the highlands between the various watershed lines, underlay the cohesion of the moundbuilding region. (Courtesy of Johns Hopkins University Press.)

0   100   200   300
Scale of Miles

much more diverse and rich array of resources for the people who lived there than did the more common temperate forests of Eurasia. Food was plentiful, even before A.D. 700, when peoples of the moundbuilding region began to depend upon corn and other domesticated plants for a large part of their food supply. Wild plants provided numerous edible seeds and highly nutritious nuts and berries, and wild animals and fish provided an ample source of meat. When people from the Eastern Hemisphere first arrived, deer were still so numerous that they roamed in great herds. The supply of bear meat and wild turkey was abundant. Early European travelers reported that the rivers were filled with monstrous fish, some so large that they threatened to overturn their canoes. And during those seasons when birds were migrating, flocks flew overhead that were so large that they darkened the sky. As late as 1810, a traveler remarked upon a flock of passenger pigeons (now extinct) that had come to rest in a willow grove near where the Ohio River flows into the Mississippi. They blanketed a forty-acre area, and were so densely perched that branches broke off from the trees and saplings bent to a ground covered with dung and feathers.[7]

Thus in terms of such basic human needs as water, food, and shelter, this region was an abundant provider. It is, therefore, not surprising that prior to 1492 it was the most populous place north of the Valley of Mexico. Nor is it surprising that such a network of waterways, in combination with important overland trails, linked together one of the Western Hemisphere's earliest and largest exchange networks.

Nevertheless, most Americans are unaware of this past and of the mounds in their midst. We learn, instead, that soon after the Spaniards came to the Western Hemisphere, they seized the centers of the Aztec and Inca realms and thereby facilitated their conquests of Mexico and Peru. Few realize that there was one place, at least, where the Native Americans defeated the Spanish—this moundbuilding region of Eastern North America. Between 1513 and 1574, the Spanish launched a series of expeditions into what they called "Florida," the entire southeastern portion of what is now the United States. The expeditions of Juan Ponce de León (1513 and 1521), Pánfilo de Narváez (1528–1536), and Hernando de Soto (1539–1543) are well known, but what is not always made clear in our history books is that these three, as well as many of the others, ended in disaster for the Spaniards.

Both of Ponce de León's expeditions were forced to retreat to Cuba, where, after the second one, de León died of a wound. The Narváez expedition, with its five ships carrying about 600 men, was quite comparable in size to those that took Mexico and Peru. But it succumbed to storms, illness, mismanagement, and sustained Native American resistance. After the Spaniards had to abandon their position on the mainland, many of the men were lost at sea; on land, only four survived to make a retreat into the Spanish-held portion of Mexico.[8]

De Soto's forces (which numbered 600 soldiers and 220 horses at the beginning) also suffered heavy losses. After de Soto's death from a fever on the Mississippi in 1542, only about 300 of his men were able to make a successful retreat by sea and find their way to Spanish territory in Mexico[9]. It was not until 1574 that the Spaniards had a secure position even on the Florida peninsula. Thereafter they abandoned their efforts to conquer the rest of "Florida" and concentrated on maintaining the security of the Bahama Channel.

No doubt, there were many reasons why the expeditions of de León, de Narváez, and de Soto did not turn out like those of Cortés and Pizarro. Among them, one of the most important was that in Eastern North America there was no single center which the Spaniards could capture and thereby seize an empire, as they did in Mexico and in the Andes. Nor were there peoples recently subjugated by a single center, who would willingly ally with an outsider for an assault upon the hated conqueror. While it is true that Cahokia had been preeminent some three hundred years before, even at the peak of its influence it had been one of several important centers. In any case its power was gone long before the sixteenth century. At the time of the Spanish incursions, the moundbuilding region was home to a number of contending powers, and although a few of its rulers entertained hopes of enlisting the Europeans against their rivals, the Spaniards were unable to sustain any alliances for long.

The absence of an all-conquering power, however, did not mean that the region was lacking in military might. Its peoples did, after all, defeat the Spaniards, sometimes acting alone and sometimes in concert, and the Spaniards were impressed by the number and the skill of the warriors who mobilized against them. When the de Soto expedition was on the Mississippi River, for example, it encountered a fleet of two hundred large dugout canoes, each filled with many men. The warriors stood with their bows and arrows at the ready, while others sheltered the oarsmen with feathered shields. The leader of the expedition sat under an awning, on a raised platform at the rear of a barge, and from this perch gave orders to the rest of the force. According to one of the expedition's chroniclers, the fleet "appeared like a famous armada of galleys."[10]

Had the Spaniards been able to conquer a significant portion of the moundbuilding region, the later history of Eastern North America would certainly have been different. To understand why the Native American peoples from this region were able to defeat them, it is necessary to know something about their precontact customs and organization. It was their past that influenced the manner in which they approached the newcomers, and it contributed to the outcome of those encounters as well. Events that transpired before 1492 thus had an impact on those after the arrival of peoples from the Eastern Hemisphere, when American history is usually deemed to begin. But even if this were not the case, and the peoples of the moundbuilding region had not played an important role in shaping postcontact events in this and many other ways, their story would still be important. It reveals the uniqueness of this land, the ingenuity of its peoples, and the diversity of the human experience. It deserves to be told, as a part of both American and world history. Without it, our history is incomplete.

2 THE ARCHAIC CONTEXT FROM WHICH MOUNDBUILDING EMERGED

Circa 8000 to 1500 B.C.

The people who built the mounds in Eastern North America had deep roots in the region. Their moundbuilding activities were, from the very beginning, closely related to a larger complex of regional development, and this regional context was the product of various processes that can be traced back to the end of the Ice Age and the beginning of the Archaic Period (around 8000 to 500 B.C.). Global warming was transforming the planet's weather, and as the climate of Eastern North America changed, so did the plant and animal population and the shape of the land and the rivers. People throughout the region adapted to these changes, took advantage of the opportunities they offered, and thereby embarked upon the path that ultimately led to the creation of moundbuilding centers such as the one at Poverty Point, which emerged in northeastern Louisiana around 1500 B.C.

The Ice Age Hunters and Gatherers

According to the most recent archaeological findings, there were people in Eastern North America by about 12,000 B.C. This early date comes from the Meadowcroft Rockshelter in southwestern Pennsylvania. Until recently, human habitation at this site was dated to 10,000 B.C. The latest studies of material from the site, however, have pushed this date back another two thousand years.[1] These people were nomadic Ice Age hunters and gatherers, who for several thousand years used a heavy thrusting spear to hunt large animals such as the mammoth and the mastodon, as well as small- and medium-size animals such as rabbits, caribou, and bison (buffalo). They lived together in small and highly mobile groups and followed the movements of the big game for long distances. Plants also provided a part of their diet, since they were able to gather nuts, berries, and edible seeds as they moved from one location to another.

Around 9000 B.C. the mammoth and the mastodon became extinct, and in the Western Hemisphere so did the horse and the camel. The dramatic demise of these animals has led some archaeologists to speculate that their extinction in North America was due to overhunting. However, most archaeologists today do not believe that this is the best explanation. The mass extinction of large Ice Age species was a worldwide phenomenon and was most likely the result of climatic changes. The first signs of global warming began around 14,000 B.C. By 12,000 B.C. the glaciers of the Ice Age began to recede and the earth's climatic patterns began to change in significant ways. As a result, these large animals suffered a massive loss of habitat as warmer and drier weather conditions transformed the places where they had once flourished.

Localization Begins after 8000 B.C.

The beginning of the Archaic Period around 8000 B.C. coincides with the retreat of the ice sheet from the Great Lakes Region. The people in Eastern North America remained hunters and gatherers, but they began to adapt to a progressively warmer and more diverse woodland environment. Since the large game animals were extinct, there was no longer any reason to be constantly on the move. Instead, people tended to remain within a certain, defined territory, and the hunters began to depend upon forest mammals such as the white-tailed deer. The process of localization had begun. People became more familiar with their own locale and its special features, adapted to it, and learned how to manipulate its environment and take advantage of the opportunities that it provided. And while engaged in this process, the people in each locale tended to become distinct from the others.

At the same time that localization occurred, there were important changes in the number and kinds of tools used. Sometime between 8000 and 7000 B.C., as the transition from Ice Age to Archaic patterns took place, the heavy thrusting spear was replaced by the atlatl (Illustration 1; illustrations follow page 50). This new weapon had three parts: a relatively lightweight spear (sometimes referred to as a javelin), a throwing stick with a notch on one end, and a banner stone. The banner stone (Illustration 2) had a hole drilled through it so that it could be slipped over the throwing stick. The spear was placed on the stick with its back end up against the notch. The hunter then used the throwing stick to hurl the spear. Apparently, the weight of the banner stone on the throwing stick gave a hunter more leverage and increased the force with which the spear was propelled. The lighter spear of the atlatl was appropriate for hunting the medium- and small-size animals that were the prey of the Archaic period, and it could be thrown much further and faster than the thrusting spear. People also developed a wide variety of specialized devices for fishing and hunting, including bone fishing hooks, traps, nets, and decoys.

Icehouse Bottom, an Early Archaic site in eastern Tennessee, has also revealed tools used to process, store, and consume the local harvest of wild plants and animals. Archaeologists have found tools for the making and sharpening of stone cutting edges, the processing of carcasses and hides, and the working of bone and wood. They have also found stones for processing nuts as well as mortars and pestles for grinding seeds and nuts into pastes or flours. Technically well-made baskets, bags, clothing, and mats—items that usually do not survive— have left their impressions in clay surfaces. Some of the Early Archaic tools found at the Koster site on the Illinois River include bone awls (hole-punchers) and needles, presumably used in making leather goods. And the number and type of adzes (a stone with a chopping edge on one side and a U-shaped gouging edge on the other) suggest that dugout canoe manufacture also began in the Early Archaic Period.[2]

During the process of localization, people acquired an intimate knowledge of the local plants and animals. Many thousands of years later when European travelers arrived, they were amazed by the Native Americans' knowledge of animal behavior and by their botanical expertise. It has been estimated that long before 1492, Native Americans had some special use for "at least twenty per cent of the available vascular plants." In the Great Lakes area, for example, they "were using 275 species of plants for medicine, 130 species for food, 31 species as magical charms, 27 species for smoking, 25 species as dyes, 18 species in beverages and as flavoring, and 52 species for other various utilitarian purposes." And at sites such as Lamoka Lake in New York, "the people fed on 28 species of mammals, 13 species of birds, turtles, and at least 5 species of fish, in addition to a substantial amount of native plant food."[3]

In this regard, the Cherokees, whose precontact ancestors were a part of the moundbuilding region, have a legend that acknowledges

Native American botanical knowledge and explains why it is that there is so much medicine in plants. According to the story, there once was a time when the human population was multiplying. This caused the animals to become angry. Humans were taking up the whole earth, crowding the animals and hunting them. The animals decided to retaliate by inflicting a multitude of ailments (such as rheumatism and arthritis) upon the humans. The plants, however, thought this act of revenge was too harsh. They sympathized with the humans and came to their rescue, each one of them offering some medicinal remedy.[4]

Development of Sedentary Habits after 6000 B.C.

One of the most unusual things about the Eastern North Americans who lived within what would become the moundbuilding region is that they developed a sedentary way of life long before they developed any dependence upon domesticated plants for their food supply. It is sometimes assumed that people who acquire their food by hunting wild animals and gathering wild plants must migrate from place to place in order to find enough to eat. But this was not the case in what became the moundbuilding region. During the Middle Archaic Period, from roughly 6000 to 3000 B.C., people began to establish permanent settlements.

This development seems to have been closely linked to continued global warming. Ocean levels had long been rising, and by 6000 B.C. the water level in the river valleys had also risen. The rivers' courses were no longer so steep, and the flow of the water had slowed. They began to meander, especially the long ones, to accumulate silt in their flood plains, and to form backwater lakes and marshes. This provided an environment in which freshwater shellfish such as mussels and bottom fish flourish, and this abundant and reliable food supply attracted people to the river valleys.

When establishing permanent settlements, people showed a strong preference for highlands that were located in or near flood plains where aquatic resources were concentrated. These sites often are marked by large shell middens. (A midden is a deposit of debris, left behind by humans.) By 4500 B.C. people tended to remain at such settlements for most of the year. Indeed, it appears that at some locations, such as the Black Earth site (Carrier Mills, in southern Illinois), there was permanent, year-round settlement. Studies done at the Koster site in southern Illinois indicate that although it was fish that drew people to these locations, the inhabitants nevertheless ate significant amounts of other foods. Judging from the bones left behind, deer ribs were a popular item, and people also ate large quantities of hickory nuts (a highly nutritious food, rich in protein and oil).

The change in habitat and subsistence patterns was most characteristic of the Mississippi River woodland drainage north of the thirty-fourth parallel (which runs about seventy miles south of Memphis, Tennessee). It was especially significant within the drainage basins of the Mississippi's more northern tributaries, including the Ohio, the Tennessee, and the Missouri. There were also important sites within the Atlantic drainage of the Southeast, on the Savannah River (now the border between South Carolina and Georgia) and along the St. Johns River in northeastern Florida. The sites in the Mississippi drainage are several thousand years older than those in the Southeast. Nevertheless, it is possible that shell midden sites developed at roughly the same time in both places, but that the earliest ones in the Southeast have not been found by archaeologists because they were submerged as the water level in the Atlantic rose. The modern coastline did not stabilize at its present level until sometime around 2500 B.C.

There are also a number of sites where the trend toward a sedentary way of life can be seen in home construction. By about 5000 B.C. people at the Koster site, for example, began to build sturdy homes meant to last for years. They were 20 to 25 feet long and 12 to 15 feet wide. During the construction process, the builders first created a flat surface by cutting terraces into the slope of a hill. Next they dug a trench and set large tree trunks (some ten inches in diameter) into it to form the frame of the house. They filled in the space between the posts with saplings, which were bent over to form a roof. The trenches were then filled to keep the posts and saplings in place, and clay was used to fill in the walls. The roof was covered with bark, but the two ends of the house were left open. Archaeologists believe that in the summer, people used grass mats to cover the ends, and that during the winters they covered them with thick animal skins. Trenches were also dug around the house to provide drainage so that water did not seep in at floor level.[5]

Exchange Networks and Elites after 3000 B.C.

Between 3000 and 1500 B.C., during the first fifteen hundred years of the Late Archaic Period (3000 to 500 B.C.), there were a number of new developments in the region. Rainfall and humidity were increasing, and people became ever more firmly tied to the permanent settlements established in river and stream valley locations. They tended to remain at these sites for a greater part of each year and eventually chose to inhabit them for three seasons of every year, from spring to autumn. It was only during the winter hunting season that they maintained small base camps in the forested highlands between the river valleys. Between 3000 and 1500 B.C., the region also witnessed the development of long-distance exchange networks, the formation of elites, the appearance of pottery, the beginnings of horticulture, and a significant increase in population.

The long-distance exchange networks that developed after 3000 B.C. were in part the result of the localization that had occurred during the early and middle parts of the Archaic Period. Becoming tied to a specific place had its advantages and its disadvantages. Localization made it possible to identify and develop local specialties, but it also made it more difficult to acquire resources from far-off places.

In particular, people were interested in acquiring specific kinds of stones, such as various kinds of flint from which the sharpest cutting edges could be made. They were also interested in shells and mineral ores that might serve either ceremonial or utilitarian purposes. Although there were only a few places with ample supplies of these goods, the demand for them grew, and the result was the emergence of long-distance exchange networks.

Sometime around 3000 B.C., for the first time in the entire Western Hemisphere, people began to exploit copper deposits. These deposits were in the vicinity of Lake Superior, in Wisconsin, Upper Michigan, and Ontario, Canada. The most important sites were at Keewenaw Peninsula and Isle Royal (both in Lake Superior in Upper Michigan), where easily accessible veins yielded large nuggets of almost pure copper. The metal was heated and hammered into various tools: awls for making small holes in leather or wood, projectile points for the tips of spears, knives, scrapers, hooks, gouges, adzes, and drills. It was also made into beads, and after 1000 B.C. into a number of decorative items. Copper tools have been found in Late Archaic sites along the Missouri River as far west as the Dakotas and in the Ohio River drainage; and small amounts have been found in New England and the Southeast. But most of these tools have been found in areas adjacent to the Great Lakes. The highest concentration of finds has been in eastern Wisconsin, where by 1904 over 13,000 copper artifacts had been recovered, mostly by farmers with Late Archaic sites on their property.[6]

Galena, a lead sulphide ore, also became a significant exchange item all along the Mississippi River during this period. With the exception of only three sites, one in Missouri and two on the Gulf coast in Mississippi and Florida, it has been found only at sites in the vicinity of the Mississippi River, from present-day southern Wisconsin to Louisiana. Although natural deposits of galena can be found in a number of places within the moundbuilding region, there were two sources of particular significance. One, referred to as the Upper Mississippi Valley, is located where Illinois, Iowa, and Wisconsin meet; and the other, often called Potosi, is in southeastern Missouri, near where the Ohio River meets the Mississippi.

Galena was usually ground into a fine powder and used to make sparkling powder or a silvery white body paint. During the Late Archaic Period, it seems to have become closely associated with ceremonial activity, since unusually large quantities of the crushed ore have been found at mound sites. After 200 B.C., the use of galena would spread throughout the moundbuilding region, where it could be found as crushed ore or in the form of beads and cones.[7]

Hematite, sometimes referred to as red ochre, is an iron oxide ore. This ore, which came from Upper Michigan, can be found in Late Archaic sites in Wisconsin, Illinois, and Indiana, as well as in the Lower Mississippi Valley. Because of its density, it was used to make plummets, or weights, for fishing nets. And it was also ground into powder in order to make a red pigment, which was sometimes used to make body paint. (In the postcontact period, some Native American peoples used red paint to draw around their own eyes the markings that surround a falcon's eyes. In so doing, they hoped to appropriate the hunting skills of this bird. Since the paint probably reduced the glare of the sun or the snow, it may well have improved their eyesight and their ability to spot their prey.)

The formation of elites also marks the Late Archaic Period. In earlier periods, grave sites and burials reveal no significant distinctions among people other than age or gender. However, after 3000 B.C. a few people were treated differently. They were interred in elaborate graves and in a manner that suggests special ceremonies. These elite burials contain a wide variety of exchange goods from distant places. For example, those in Wisconsin, Illinois, and Indiana have been found to contain hematite, copper beads and awls, beads made from Gulf of Mexico shells, tubular pipes, banner stones shaped like birds, and ground slate ornaments.

Indian Knoll, located on Kentucky's Green River near where it enters the Ohio, was one of the largest shell midden sites of the period. Even though this site is not usually thought of as one showing status differentiation, about 4 percent of the burials yielded exotic exchange items, including copper and goods made from marine shells. There are also graves in which women and children were buried with atlatls. Since these weapons could not have been their personal possessions, their presence suggests that there was some sort of rank distinction and that these weapons marked the members of a privileged family or lineage.

The Earliest Pottery Appears around 2500 B.C.

The oldest pottery ever found anywhere in North America (including Mexico) is from a site on Stallings Island, South Carolina, in the Savannah River, not far from Savannah, Georgia. This handformed, fiber-tempered ware has been dated to 2515 B.C. (Clay objects are prone to cracking and other problems when fired. The likelihood of such problems occurring is reduced if potters begin by mixing substances such as crushed fibers or sand into the clay in order to temper it.) By about 2000 B.C., similar pots could be found to the south, in sites along Florida's Atlantic coast. By 1300 B.C., clay objects could be found in the Lower Mississippi Valley, and by 1000 B.C., pottery could be found in many places throughout Florida.

The sites along the Savannah River and on Florida's Atlantic coast were shell midden sites where both freshwater and marine shellfish were abundant. The largest part of the peoples' diet (30 percent), nevertheless, was wild plant food. Deer made up 24.2 percent, and snails provided another 24 percent. Small mammals, birds, and fish made up the rest. By 2000 B.C. the peoples who lived in Florida's shell midden sites appear not only to have been sedentary but to have lived in the same place throughout the year. Before 1200 B.C. they made shallow, flat-bottomed bowls and rectangular vessels that were hand-formed and tempered exclusively with plant fibers, but thereafter the pots were tempered with a mixture of fiber and sand, and by 500 B.C. the pottery in Florida was all sand-tempered.[8]

Population Growth and the Domestication
of Plants after 2300 B.C.

Although there clearly was some relationship between population growth and plant domestication in those river valleys where people maintained relatively permanent settlements, the nature of that relationship remains unclear. It is impossible to say with any assurance which process came first. And the matter is further complicated by the fact that until 500 B.C., when the Archaic Period came to an end, people still relied primarily upon undomesticated species. Domesticated plants do not seem to have provided a significant amount of the food supply.

An increase in the number and size of sites suggests that there was a substantial increase in population during the years from 3000 to 1500 B.C. Evidence from the Koster site on the Illinois River also suggests that after 3000 B.C. life expectancy may have lengthened, since some of the skeletons unearthed from the period are those of people aged sixty, sixty-five, and even seventy. Evidence from the same site also suggests that more food was being processed, since grinding tools were improved at about the same time.

Yet the bottle gourd (*Lagenaria siceraria*), often thought to be the first domesticated plant present in the Eastern Woodlands, was grown not for food but for the purpose of making containers. It is easy to grow and reproduces readily. And after the gourds are cleaned and dried, they can be made into a wide variety of useful items. Less breakable and much lighter than clay, they were used in Eastern North America in the precontact period to make water vessels, dippers, ladles, cups, bowls, bird houses, rattles, and masks. And in Florida, peoples who fished in the deep seas used them to make floats for their fishing nets. A second early domesticate, often associated with the bottle gourd, was a species of squash (*Cucurbita pepo*). Although the seeds from some varieties of this plant are edible, it also may have been grown as a container plant.

So far, the earliest evidence of the domesticated forms of these plants in Eastern North America comes from Phillips Spring, Missouri, where they have been dated to 2300 B.C. Since they were present in Mesoamerica at a considerably earlier date, they may have been introduced to the Eastern Woodlands from the south. However, there are some archaeologists who argue that they were independently domesticated in Eastern North America, along with the sunflower (*Helianthus annuus*), which was garnered in the Great Plains, and goosefoot (*Chenopodium berlandieri*), which was indigenous to the Eastern Woodlands.

Based upon a noticeable progression in seed size and other desirable characteristics, these archaeologists suggest that as early as 4500 B.C. people had begun to manipulate the plants around them in order to encourage the growth of wild sunflowers, goosefoot, and marsh elder or sumpweed (*Iva annua macrocarpus*). Such encouragement probably included collecting and moving around the seeds of these plants, weeding out undesired competitors, and casting seeds on fertile, exposed sandbanks. By 2000 B.C. the seed characteristics of sunflowers and goosefoot suggest that they had become domesticated plants, purposefully planted, tended, and harvested. And by A.D. 1 the same would be true for marsh elder.

How effective this manipulation of plants had become by 3000 B.C., when significant population growth began, is not clear, and thus it is impossible to say that the latter was an outgrowth of the former. What *is* clear is that the peoples of the Eastern Woodlands did independently domesticate a considerable number of plants. In addition to the previously mentioned sunflower, goosefoot, and marsh elder, these included giant ragweed (*Ambrosia trifidia*), maygrass (*Phalaris caroliniana*), pigweed (*Amaranthus sp.*), smartweed or knotweed (*Polygonum erectum*), lambs-quarter (*Chenopodium sp.*), canary grass (*Phalaris canariensis*), and little barley (*Hordeum pusillum*).[9] Although the sunflower is the only one that is still an important source of food in today's world, the role played by Eastern North American peoples in the plant domestication process should not be overlooked.

Peoples in Eastern North America had no domesticated animals for any purpose, with the one exception of dogs. They were, in this respect, typical of the Western Hemisphere, where the domestication of plants was rarely accompanied by the domestication of animals. While peoples of the Eastern Hemisphere ensured their supply of meat by domesticating animals, such as pigs, chickens, and sheep, and domesticated horses, donkeys, and eventually camels for transportation, this did not happen in the Western Hemisphere. In the Andes there was a domesticated guinea pig raised for food, and there were domesticated llamas and alpacas kept for transport purposes. And in Mesoamerica and adjacent areas, people ate several domesticated birds, including the turkey. These few instances of animal domestication are the only ones in the entire hemisphere.

Even though people in North and South America used a wide variety of animal products for food, shelter, clothing, tools, and ornament, they appear to have been uninterested in domesticating the animals that provided these products. Apparently, there were abundant and accessible supplies that could be managed in the wild. People devoted themselves almost exclusively to the domestication of plants, and their accomplishments in this regard in Mesoamerica and the Andes were unsurpassed anywhere in the world.

In the absence of domesticated animals, people in Eastern North America had only two ways to travel or move cargo—they could either go on foot, carrying their loads, or they could go by canoe. Given the intricate network of waterways in the Mississippi and Gulf Coast drainages, the canoe was the obvious choice. Except in the most northern areas, these canoes were not the familiar birchbark variety. Throughout most of what would become the moundbuilding region, the typical vessel was a dugout canoe. It was made by hollowing out a large log and streamlining its bottom, a method that produced a large, strong, and speedy carrier.

The absence of any domesticated herds also meant that the peoples of Eastern North America, and in the Western Hemisphere generally, remained relatively free of infectious diseases.[10] During the Ice Age, infectious diseases could not survive among human populations in either hemisphere, since people were not concentrated in sufficient numbers to sustain such diseases. If a contagious and deadly disease appeared, it quickly killed off all its available hosts, and then it too died out since it had no more hosts to keep it alive. Large herds of wild animals, on the other hand, could sustain such diseases. Much later, when people in the Eastern Hemisphere began to keep herds of domesticated animals, they came into close contact with the animals. The humans then became infected with the diseases previously carried only by the animals, and by this time there were enough humans to keep the diseases going, and they then became human diseases.

Since such herds were not domesticated in the Western Hemisphere, infectious diseases were not transferred from animal to human populations in the Americas. Although tuberculosis does seem to have been present in Native American populations prior to 1492, it is unlikely that its transmission from animal to human populations occurred in this hemisphere. Long before 12,000 B.C., when the Bering Land Bridge between Siberia and Alaska was submerged, it was already an old disease, and it did not immediately kill off its hosts. It probably was introduced to the Western Hemisphere by Ice Age hunters who carried it across the land bridge.

Native Americans did have other sorts of diseases before 1492 that are not communicable between humans. For example, they had degenerative diseases such as rheumatism and arthritis, and they had ailments caused by parasites. But in the absence of almost all infectious diseases, it was possible for the population of Eastern North America to grow relatively unchecked by disease, and for people to live in places with concentrated populations without suffering from epidemics.

The stage was thus set for the emergence of the first moundbuilding culture. In the process of adapting to changes in climate and habitat, people had become increasingly sedentary and had developed local specialties. After 6000 B.C., many of the river valleys in the region provided such an abundance of easily accessible wild but high-quality plant and animal food that at least some people were able to establish permanent settlements and build sturdy homes, prior to the presence of any domesticated plants. After 3000 B.C. the population increased, people began to exchange their own specialties for those of others, an elite began to emerge, and domesticated plants appeared. And given the relative absence of infectious diseases, it was possible for people to engage in extensive interaction and to live in areas of population concentration without endangering their health.

3 POVERTY POINT, THE FIRST MOUNDBUILDING EPOCH

Circa 1500 to 700 B.C.

The Poverty Point Cultural Area

Eastern North America's first moundbuilding cultural area emerged during the Late Archaic Period in the Lower Mississippi Valley. The Poverty Point site, which was occupied from about 1500 to 700 B.C., was its major center. It is located in northeastern Louisiana near the town of Epps, about twelve miles west of the present course of the Mississippi River. In the nineteenth century it was part of a plantation called Poverty Point, and today archaeologists call both the center and the culture by this unfortunate name. The Poverty Point site, nevertheless, is rich both in size and significance. It is roughly three square miles in area, and millions of artifacts were contained within it. Furthermore, it is of great antiquity. It had reached its peak size by 1000 B.C., which makes it by far the oldest cultural center within the bounds of the United States, and one of the oldest centers in all North America, since it is as old as, if not older than, the well-known Olmec sites in Mexico.

The Poverty Point site is situated on the eastern edge of the Macon Ridge, a large bluff that stands about twenty feet higher than the surrounding land. It overlooks the Bayou Macon, the river that now flows along the eastern edge of the bluff on its way to the Red River and the Mississippi. (*Bayou* is a Choctaw word for "river," and *macon* is a French spelling of a Spanish word that means "large tableland.") Three thousand years ago, when Poverty Point was at its peak, low-lying marshes surrounded the bluff, and a branch of the Arkansas River flowed past its eastern side, where it formed a large lake. A branch of the Mississippi River was only eight miles to the east.

28

Some of the artifacts and ways of life that distinguish what is now known as Poverty Point culture began to appear in the area as early as 3000 B.C., and others were added gradually over the next fifteen hundred years. It thus acquired a recognizable set of tools and other manufactures that eventually included clay cooking balls, clay figurines, small drill-like tools called microflints, plummet-like objects, and small, beautifully carved stone beads, figurines, and pendants (Illustration 3).[1] The oldest earthen mound in the area, tentatively dated to around 2500 B.C., is at Banana Bayou, near the Louisiana coast.[2] Development did not begin at the Poverty Point site until about 1500 B.C., but by 1000 B.C. it had come to enjoy an unparalleled preeminence within the cultural area that now bears its name.

The Mounds at Poverty Point

The Poverty Point site is marked by earthen embankments that form six concentric semicircles, each about six feet high. (See Map 4.) The open half of the semicircle is on the east, and the distance from the northern to the southern tip of the outermost embankment is about 1,200 meters, or about three-quarters of a mile. The width of the embankments varies between 50 and 150 feet, and the swales, the spaces between them, are of about the same size. A plaza of about 37 acres occupied the space enclosed by the embankments and the river.[3] The four aisles that cut through the embankments may have served as a solar calendar. Two of them point north and south, one marks the path of the sun's rays at sunset on the summer solstice, and one does the same for the winter solstice.[4]

West of the embankments is a bird-shaped effigy mound (Mound A) that was once seventy feet high. An effigy mound is an earthwork with the shape of an animal, such as a bird or a snake, or a part of an animal, such as a bear's claw. Most are so large that the whole of the image can be seen only from the air. From the top of observation towers, where they are available, or in aerial photographs, they look like figures sculpted in high relief. At Poverty Point, the bird's head points toward the west, and the wings extend on the north–south axis with a span of over 640 feet. From head to tail it was once 710 feet long. The bird has lost some of its height since several generations of farmers plowed its top surface, and part of the tail was destroyed when a construction crew dug it up and used it as the substratum of a highway that runs through the site.

Map 4. **The Poverty Point Site.** This map, generously provided by archaeologist Jon L. Gibson, shows the six semicircular, concentric embankments and various other earthenworks that mark the three-square-mile Poverty Point site. The first important moundbuilding center in Eastern North America, it was at its peak for some three hundred years, from about 1000 to 700 B.C.

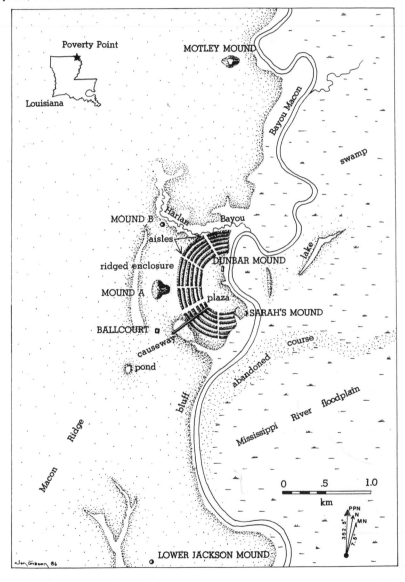

Although some of the mounds at Poverty Point have been destroyed, a number are still visible to a person standing atop the large bird-shaped mound. Some 700 yards due north is a conical mound (Mound B), and about one-and-a-half miles north of the embankments is Motley Mound. Due to a protruding lobe, some people think Motley Mound may be an unfinished bird-shaped effigy mound. Some 600 feet to the south is a square-shaped mound that is connected to the outermost embankment, and 1.6 miles to the south is the Lower Jackson Mound, which is conical in shape.

These mounds, like all those in Eastern North America, regardless of whether they belong to this epoch or to later ones, were made of earth that was dug from a nearby spot using stone tools similar to hoes. (Near the coast, shells were sometimes used in place of stone tools.) People carried this soil to its destination in baskets or leather bags. The large holes from which the earth was removed are referred to as borrow pits, and they often filled up with rain water and became ponds. There are such borrow pits at the Poverty Point site, probably dug when the various mounds where constructed, but it appears that the earth in the embankments came from the swales that lie between them.[5] The earthworks at any given site were rarely, if ever, built all at the same time, and many were built stage by stage, over a period of generations. Nevertheless, it is obvious that their construction required specialized knowledge, careful planning, and the coordination of large amounts of labor.

Population Patterns

It has been estimated that as many as 5,000 people lived at the Poverty Point site during its heyday around 1000 B.C.[6] Refuse patterns suggest that some residents built their homes on the embankments, and it is possible that like the semicircular embankments, their doors faced east. Post holes reveal that the houses were circular and measured between thirteen and fifteen feet across. There were also a number of small residential hamlets that stretched for some three miles to the north and south of the enclosed plaza. It is also possible that all the villages located on Macon Ridge and adjacent lowlands, some of which were twenty to thirty miles away, were closely connected to the Poverty Point site.

There are over one hundred sites that were once a part of the Poverty

Map 5. **The Poverty Point Cultural Area.** The Poverty Point center (marked by a star) and the nine contemporary settlement clusters shown on this map are referred to collectively as the Poverty Point cultural area because of cultural similarities among the peoples living in all ten locales.

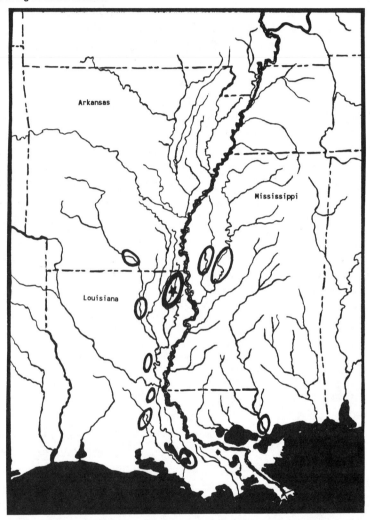

Point cultural area. They appear in ten clusters, one at Poverty Point and nine at other places in eastern Louisiana, southern Arkansas, and western Mississippi. (See Map 5.) Within these clusters the sites varied in size from less than one acre to over one hundred acres, and their populations varied from only a few families to numbers in the hundreds. Although none was in the same league as Poverty Point, in almost every cluster there was a large site marked by earthworks, usually embankments and sometimes dome-shaped mounds. In general, the number and size of the earthworks varied directly with the size of the settlement. Perhaps the best metaphor for the pattern suggested is that of a solar system. The Poverty Point site stood at the center, like a large sun. Nearby were its own small moons. Somewhat more distant, but still within its field of gravity were nine moderately sized planets, and each of these had its own set of moons.

Food Supplies

These ten population clusters were separated by considerable distances, sometimes scores of miles, an indication that the people concentrated only within certain especially desirable settings. In their choice of habitat they clearly followed the pattern that had typified parts of Eastern North America ever since the Middle Archaic Period. People sought river and stream valleys where there was high ground surrounded by large expanses of low-lying wetlands. Such locales were safe during floods and provided a generous supply of food throughout the year, and it was thus possible to establish permanent villages in these places. One also finds temporary campsites within the Lower Mississippi Valley, either used for winter hunting or to gather seasonally available foods or other resources.

These Lower Mississippi River sites, however, differ from the typical Middle Archaic pattern in that no freshwater mollusk shells have been found in them. The only shell middens appear at coastal sites, where saltwater shellfish were eaten. Those who lived away from the coast ate quantities of fish instead, especially gar, catfish, buffalo fish, and sunfish. Like others in Eastern North America, they ate an abundance of venison, and unlike most others, they sometimes ate alligators. Rabbits, opossums, raccoons, squirrels, and snakes were among the small animals they hunted for food, and they also brought home turkeys, cranes, and other kinds of birds.

Their nut larder included hickory nuts, pecans, acorns, and walnuts, and they also ate persimmons, wild grapes, wild beans, and hackberries. Plant residue in Lower Mississippi Valley sites has not yet been studied as extensively as that in more northern sites, but honey locust, goosefoot, knotweed, and other seeds have been found. Some of the sites in the Poverty Point cultural area have produced evidence of the cultivation of domesticated plants, or at least the management and encouragement of sunflowers, sumpweed, goosefoot, and others that produce large quantities of nutritional seeds.[7] There is also some evidence for the cultivation of bottle gourds and squash, both for their edible seeds and for containers.[8]

Poverty Point Manufactures

The people of Poverty Point produced a wide variety of finely crafted objects. As early as 1300 B.C. they began to work with clay. Within the Mississippi River drainage basin, they were not only the first but the only ones to do so before about 500 B.C. They made bowls and other vessels, but mostly they made cooking balls. In Eastern North America food was often roasted over a fire or wrapped in some material such as leaves and put directly on hot coals, but before the appearance of large clay pots suitable for stewing, it was impossible to make a stew over a fire. People did it by placing the food and water into a tightly woven basket or leather pouch and dropping heated stones into the container.[9] Possibly because of a shortage of suitable cooking stones in the coastal areas, however, the people of the Poverty Point cultural sphere used clay balls to heat stews as well as earth ovens. An earth oven was a carefully made hole in the ground. The cook filled part of the hole with heated clay balls and then put the food in, where it would be baked by the heat that radiated from the ball. These balls come in a variety of shapes, and it has been suggested that different shapes gave off heat of a different intensity and duration, and that by manipulating the balls, the cook could adjust the heat in the oven.

Archaeologists have also found quantities of stone tools at various sites in the Poverty Point cultural area. These include spear points, atlatl weights or banner stones (including some that are boat-shaped), plummets, and what appear to be some sort of hoe. The hoe blades have a fused opal coating, which indicates that they were used to cut through sod. They tend to be found in villages rather than at centers, and they are most abundant at the Terral Lewis site, a small hamlet about ten miles southeast of the Poverty Point site. Another tool found at numerous Poverty Point sites is a microflint. There is no certainty regarding how it was used, but one possibility is that it was a small drill used to make holes in other stones. And since 91 percent of the microflints found at the Poverty Point site are concentrated in its southern and southwestern sectors, it would seem that an artisan community was concentrated only in certain neighborhoods of this center.[10]

Many of the most interesting objects made within the Poverty Point cultural area were for personal adornment or enjoyment, or for ceremonial use. Red jasper (a quartz) appears to have been the preferred material. Claw-shaped pendants and small owls were often made from it, and red jasper beads are also numerous. One of the most curious beads is a locust, so beautifully carved that even this insect is endowed with a certain charm (Illustration 4). There are also small clay figurines which may be fertility symbols, since some of them appear to be pregnant women. Some researchers have suggested that the objects of personal adornment were marks of social distinction. If so, their presence in such large quantities at Poverty Point–related sites would indicate that there was more stratification within this area than elsewhere at the time.

Sites in the Poverty Point cultural area also have yielded pipes, the first to be found in the southeast. The best were made of stone, but clay pipes seem to have been considered an acceptable substitute. At the time of contact between Europe and America, pipes were used in ceremonies to declare war or celebrate friendship and alliance between different peoples, but it is not known whether such uses date back to the Late Archaic Period at Poverty Point. Although by no means certain, it is possible that tobacco was smoked in Poverty Point pipes. Tobacco (*Nicotiana rustica*) was one of several plants smoked in Eastern North America at the time of contact. It is a South American domesticate, and it may have reached Eastern North America, at least in small amounts, during the Late Archaic Period. The oldest tobacco seeds so far identified in the region were discovered in Illinois, and one of them was found in a site dated to 1200 B.C.[11]

Poverty Point Exchange Networks

The peoples of Eastern North America were truly connoisseurs of stones and minerals. Although there were sources of similar materials relatively nearby, much of the raw material used to manufacture stone objects at Poverty Point was imported from places that were many hundreds of miles away, apparently because the imported materials were of a better quality or were more attractive than the local product. There seems to have been a strong demand for various kinds of flint, including chert. These stones can be chipped to take on sharp edges, and they were thus the preferred material for cutting tools and spear points. Steatite (soapstone) and sandstone are soft and were shaped into bowls and grinding basins. Hematite and magnetite are heavy and could be made into carefully shaped weights, or plummets, and attached to fishing nets or bolas (a weapon used to entangle an animal's feet).

Since most of the imports were bulky and heavy, the easiest way to transport them would have been by canoe, and thus there was a clear advantage to being downstream from the best sources. In this respect the Poverty Point cultural area was in an ideal position to amass the finest in raw materials: close to the Mississippi River, well below the point that the Ohio and the Tennessee join it. Materials could also be brought downstream from the Ozark Mountains on the Arkansas and Ouachita rivers. Imports to the area included copper and slate from the Great Lakes area, gray northern flint from the Ohio River valley, and schist and Pickwick chert from the Tennessee River Valley and northern Georgia.

Tons of southern Appalachian steatite also reached the Poverty Point area. It may have come down the Tennessee River and then the Mississippi, or it may have come by way of the Gulf coast. Some 200 to 300 steatite vessels were found buried in an oval pit southwest of the Poverty Point site's bird-shaped mound, and similar bowl burials have been found on the Gulf coast near New Orleans in a Poverty Point–related site.[12]

Some galena came from the Upper Mississippi Valley, but most of it came from the Potosi site in southern Missouri. (So much galena has been uncovered at the Poverty Point site and nearby that it has been suggested that Poverty Point people themselves went to the Missouri site to exploit this ore.)[13] The Ozarks supplied Ozark chert, Black Bighorn chert, novaculite, hematite, and magnetite, and quartz and fluorite also came down the Ouachita. Red jasper, greenstone, quartzite, and granite came from eastern Mississippi, and may have arrived by overland routes or by way of the Gulf of Mexico. The Poverty Point site also imported Pebble chert, Catahoula sandstone, and Yellow Pebble chert from within its own cultural area.

One of the most interesting studies of this Late Archaic mound-building sphere has revealed the internal movement of goods, local and imported. The Poverty Point site was clearly the hub of the system, even though it was not located at the area's geographical center, but at the common junction of the most important rivers. And given that all the other sites are on or near rivers, it appears that the transport of goods between this hub and other sites was also by river. Unlike any other cluster or site in the area, Poverty Point received a portion of every item imported into its sphere. A part of its share was worked at the site, and many of the finished goods are also to be found there and in its surrounding hamlets. It also appears that it had something approaching sole claim over a few items, for these are rarely found at any other cluster or site. Some of the more northern sites, such as Jaketown in northern Mississippi and Deep Bayou in southern Arkansas appear to have been outposts where imported materials were amassed. Only a portion of this material was taken to the Poverty Point site, and some of it moved through Poverty Point to more southern sites, either as raw material or in a partially worked form.[14]

Poverty Point appears to have exported finished goods made of stone and clay. These objects have been found in Missouri and Tennessee, along the Gulf coast, and even in northeastern Florida, in sites near the Atlantic Ocean. In the Florida sites, clay balls seem to be the most common Poverty Point items,[15] perhaps because there was a local shortage of good cooking stones in sandy coastal areas.

Poverty Point flourished for several hundred years after reaching its peak around 1000 B.C., but after 700 B.C. it lost its preeminence, and its unique style of moundbuilding faded away. Archaeologists do not yet understand why it declined. After 500 B.C. a second epoch of moundbuilding began, this time in the Ohio River valley. Several centuries thereafter, a new style of moundbuilding spread out from Ohio, and the peoples in what had once been Poverty Point's sphere would adopt new styles and ceremonies. There would be new mounds and new ways in Eastern North America's oldest cultural area.

4 ADENA-HOPEWELL, THE SECOND MOUNDBUILDING EPOCH

Circa 500 B.C. to A.D. 400

The second epoch of moundbuilding centers took place during the Woodlands Period, a millennium dated roughly from 500 B.C. to A.D. 500. The centers first appeared among peoples of the Adena culture (about 500 to 100 B.C.) in what is now central and southern Ohio, along tributaries that flow into the Ohio River. While the Adena culture was flourishing and spreading up and down the Ohio River, peoples throughout much of Eastern North America began to manufacture pottery. Around 200 B.C. a second moundbuilding culture, the Hopewell, emerged in Ohio, and soon thereafter corn-cultivating, Hopewellian-style centers appeared throughout the region. These centers were all part of an interaction sphere that merged the various exchange zones of the Late Archaic Period into a single network and created the cultural continuities that characterize the moundbuilding region.

The earthworks of the second epoch are some of the most intriguing anywhere in the world. Many sites are marked by elaborate geometric designs combining hexagons, circles, squares, and rectangles; others, especially those in Wisconsin and its vicinity, are marked by effigy mounds. Among the many shapes are birds with outspread wings, snakes, and bear claws (Illustration 5). Some of the sites are small, encompassing around ten acres, but others enclose hundreds of acres.[1] Architects and engineers today are impressed by the geometrical and astronomical sophistication that the design and construction of these mounds demonstrate. The utilitarian, ceremonial, and ornamental objects produced at this time are also finely crafted, and their design has retained its appeal across the centuries.

The Ohio River became a major thoroughfare, from its most distant headwaters in New York and Pennsylvania to southern Illinois, where it enters the Mississippi. The preeminence that it enjoyed during this epoch was still evident in 1848, when E. G. Squier and E. H. Davis published an extensive survey of North American earthenworks entitled *Ancient Monuments of the Mississippi Valley.* They noted:

> [In] the regions watered by the Ohio and its tributaries . . . we find numberless mounds. . . . These are by far the most imposing class of our aboriginal remains and impress us most sensibly with the numbers and power of the people who built them. . . . The number of [mounds] may be safely estimated at 10,000. . . . There are few sections of the country of equal extent which embrace so large a number of ancient works.[2]

Although some of the Ohio River valley mounds that they counted and surveyed are from a later period, most were constructed during this second epoch. Indeed, it was only during this epoch that moundbuilding spread all the way up this river and even beyond it, out of the Mississippi drainage and into the drainage basin of Lake Ontario.

Ohio is an Iroquois word for "beautiful." What earned the river this name were its sparkling water, its lush green islands, and the views it offered of forest-covered hills, fertile bottomlands, and brightly colored wild flowers and birds. Redbud trees bloomed in the spring, and in the fall the white bark of the sycamores gleamed. Cardinals and the red, green, and yellow Carolina parakeets (now extinct) perched in the trees. Dense flocks of geese and ducks landed on its waters, and turkeys, partridges, and quail could be seen on its shores.[3]

Pottery

During the Late Archaic Period clay objects and pottery were produced at various southern locations—on the South Atlantic coast in the vicinity of the Savannah River, in Florida, and within the Poverty Point cultural area—but they were not produced in the North. It was during the Woodland Period, sometime between 500 and 200 B.C., that a knowledge of pottery production appears to have spread from the South to the Tennessee River valley, the Central Mississippi Valley, and the Illinois Valley. Archaeologists who study the Central Mississippi Valley (between the mouths of the Ohio and the Arkansas) believe that the earliest pottery found there was imported, perhaps from the Tennessee River valley, since the earliest pieces are already sophisticated and decorated. And between A.D. 200 and 400, long after pottery was made in the North, southeastern pots were still imported into Ohio.

The production of large clay pots greatly facilitated the cooking process. Leather or reed stewing baskets could not be put directly over a fire, and the contents had to be heated with either stones or clay cooking balls such as those used at Poverty Point. The ability to make clay cooking pots made these devices unnecessary, since cooks could put the pots directly on the fire and keep them simmering throughout the day.[4]

The Adena Culture

Although the Adena culture had been present in Ohio for many centuries before, it was only after about 500 B.C. that its peoples began to construct moundbuilding centers. One of its earliest and most important sites was in the Scioto River valley near Chillicothe, Ohio. This fertile valley also drew the attention of Squier and Davis, who recognized it as "a favorite resort of the ancient people, and . . . one of the seats of their densest population."[5] Other Adena sites can be found within a radius of 150 miles of Chillicothe, on both sides of the Ohio River from Kentucky and eastern Indiana to West Virginia and western Pennsylvania. (See Map 6.)

Perhaps the most famous Adena mound is the Serpent Mound, on Brush Creek near Peebles, Ohio (Illustration 6). The distance from the snake's head to its tail is about 800 feet, but if it were stretched out to form a straight line it would measure over 1,300 feet long. When it was first measured in 1846, the body was close to 5 feet high and 30 feet wide, but due to erosion and plowing, its height is now about 4 feet and its width about 20 feet. The mouth of the snake is wide open and within it is an oval-shaped object which looks like an egg. And the end of the snake's tail winds around into a triple coil. (The object in the snake's mouth may have represented the sun, since there is a Native American legend that the sun was once swallowed by a snake.)

One of the reasons that southern Ohio gained such prominence during this epoch may well have been the stone outcroppings in its river valleys. Quarries in the Lower Scioto Valley yielded a fine-grained siltstone which was used to make tubular pipes (Illustration 7) and platform pipes, long, flat tubes with a sculpture, often an animal, perched on one end. Siltstone was an excellent material for pipemaking

Map 6. **Adena Site Locations.** A second epoch of moundbuilding began among the Adena peoples sometime after 500 B.C. Although concentrated in central and southern Ohio, Adena sites have also been found on Ohio River tributaries in Indiana, Kentucky, West Virginia, and Pennsylvania.

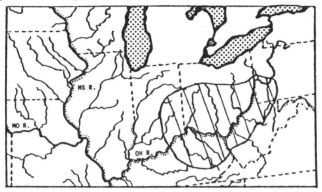

since it was easily drilled and carved and had a nice sheen when polished. As with other Adena products, the pipes were in great demand, and have been found as far away as the Chesapeake Bay area in Maryland, in New England, and in the St. Lawrence River valley in Canada.

Yet another item that first appeared in the Adena societies was a particular kind of carved stone tablet (Illustration 8). These were small flat rectangles delicately carved with abstracted snake and bird designs. Since traces of pigment have been found on some, they apparently were used to stamp designs upon some flat surface, perhaps bark cloth or deerskin. Such stone tablets have been found both in the northern portion of the Woodlands and in two places near the Gulf coast but not in any intervening places.[6]

The Hopewell Culture

Around 300 B.C., a new culture began to form in the valley of the Scioto River and also in the valleys of two other Ohio tributaries, the Muskingum and the Miami. Archaeologists refer to it as the Hopewell, for no better reason than that in the nineteenth century a man named Captain M. C. Hopewell once owned a farm on which there were some thirty mounds. The archaeologist Warren K. Moorehead dug the site and came across a large number of artifacts. In 1893 he displayed them at the Chicago World's Fair under the label "Hopewell," and the term thus became attached to an entire epoch in North American history.

The Hopewell and the Adena cultures existed side by side in southern Ohio for some time, and there seems to be little doubt that the

Hopewell emerged from the Adena. On the other hand, a number of items that are now identified as Hopewell seem to have been in southern Illinois prior to their appearance in southern Ohio, and thus some archaeologists have suggested that Hopewell developed in Ohio due to influences coming from the west. After 200 B.C. the new Hopewell culture became increasingly important, and the Adena culture gradually disappeared.

Indeed, it was the spread throughout the Eastern Woodlands of many elements from this new Hopewell culture (see Map 7) that essentially created the moundbuilding region as it is defined in Chapter 1 of this book. (The only portion of the region that the Hopewellian sphere did not include was outside the Eastern Woodlands, along the upper Missouri.) In large part, it was the Hopewellian interaction sphere that delineated the region's boundaries and gave it some of its most characteristic features. Hopewellian-style moundbuilding, mortuary customs, artifact styles, and even ritual and religious beliefs spread throughout the region, and so did corn cultivation. And a single exchange network facilitated the circulation of resources and goods.

Stoneworking at the Center

Like the people at Poverty Point and Adena sites, the Hopewellian peoples in southern Ohio also seem to have specialized in stoneworking. Hopewellian pieces from Ohio have been found throughout the moundbuilding region, even as far away as Florida. Thin, narrow, prismatic blades of chalcedony (a kind of quartz) were one of their specialties. Flint was also abundant, especially at Flint Ridge in Licking County, Ohio. It appears, however, that local stone resources could not keep up with demand, and raw materials had to be imported from other places, since unfinished pieces and discards of imported stones have been found in residential sites in Ohio, outside the ceremonial areas. Indeed, hundreds of pounds of obsidian were brought all the way from Yellowstone, down the Missouri and the Mississippi, and then up the Ohio to the Scioto Valley.[7]

The Development of a Regionwide Exchange Network

At approximately the same time that moundbuilding centers spread throughout the region, the various separate trading zones of the Late

Map 7. **The Moundbuilding Region During the Hopewellian Period (ca. 200 B.C. to A.D. 400).** This is an abbreviated version of a map prepared by the Museum of Anthropology, University of Michigan, first published in James B. Griffin, "Eastern North American Archaeology: A Summary," *Science* 156:3772, 175–91 (14 April 1967). Although the original was drawn in 1967 and thus does not reflect all that has been learned since then, it is still one of the best available maps of the region. (Copyright 1967, by the American Association for the Advancement of Science.)

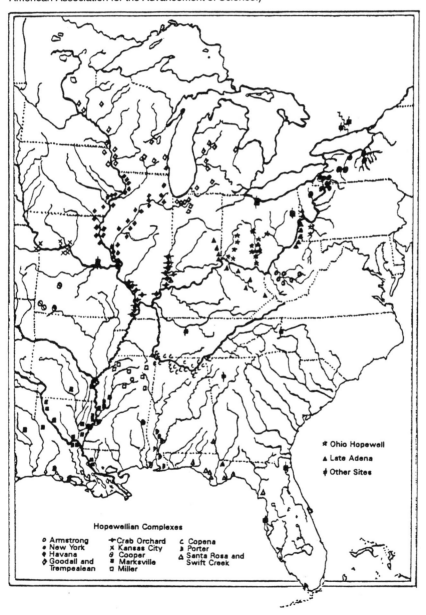

✸ Ohio Hopewell

▲ Late Adena

⧫ Other Sites

Hopewellian Complexes

○ Armstrong	✦ Crab Orchard	⊂ Copena
● New York	✕ Kansas City	▶ Porter
◆ Havana	ẟ Cooper	△ Santa Rosa and
◊ Goodall and	■ Marksville	Swift Creek
Trempealean	▢ Miller	

Archaic Period were merged into one, creating an exchange network that encompassed the entire moundbuilding region. Prior to 200 B.C., marine shells from southeastern coasts were one (and perhaps the only) long-distance exchange item that could be found throughout what became the region. For the most part, copper had been confined to an east–west belt across the north, and galena and hematite were most often found in sites along the Mississippi River. However, by about 200 B.C., these specialty items, along with many more, could be found throughout the entire Hopewellian sphere. An elaborate exchange network of nearly continental proportions had emerged, capable of amassing resources from the Rocky Mountains to the Appalachians and from the Great Lakes to the Gulf of Mexico.

Mound sites throughout the region have yielded large quantities of the same highly valued items: tens of thousands of freshwater pearls from the Mississippi and its tributaries; Great Lakes copper (found in the Archaic Period mostly as beads and tools) hammered into ear spools, pan pipes, breast plates, and various decorative forms; silver from Ontario; hematite from Michigan; chert from Illinois; Upper Mississippi Valley galena for white paint and sparkling powder (which could be obtained during this epoch either as beads or in cones); ceramic figurines from Illinois, Ohio, and Wisconsin (Illustration 9); flint blades and carved soapstone pipes from Ohio; mica from southern Appalachia (which was often separated into thin sheets and cut into artfully shaped human hands, birds, and snakes); crystalline quartz from Arkansas; obsidian, chalcedony, and bear's teeth from the Rocky Mountains; shell beads and whole marine shells, sharks' teeth, alligator teeth, barracuda jaws, and turtle shells from the Gulf of Mexico; and Gulf Coast stamped pottery (Illustrations 9 through 12).[8] Some who study this period believe that this exchange may also have included such things as animal skins and dried meat, which are perishable and thus would have left no archaeological trace.

Corn in Hopewellian Sites

Although corn of some variety appears to have been grown in both Florida and southern Georgia during the latter part of the Late Archaic Period, there was no corn in the rest of Eastern North America until the Hopewellian Period. It is only after 200 B.C. that tropical flint corn, first domesticated in Mesoamerica, can be found throughout the moundbuilding region. There was much excitement among researchers when it was first discovered, and some then theorized that its cultivation had increased the food supply and thereby made possible sedentary habits and mound construction. However, it is now clear that both sedentary habits and moundbuilding characterized the region long before the arrival of corn and that even though everyone involved in the construction of Hopewellian-style mounds grew corn, none grew it in large amounts. Nor did it become a significant part of the peoples' diets during this period. Indigenous plants, either domesticated or wild, continued to be the most important source of plant food.

Even though people grew corn only in small amounts, there is no doubt that they cultivated it for a purpose. The corn plant will not grow in the wild and is completely dependent upon farmers for its propagation. Since its production during the Hopewellian epoch seems to be closely linked to moundbuilding, it seems quite possible that it was grown especially for ceremonies performed at the mounds. During the sixteenth century when Europeans first observed moundbuilding societies, they noted that the noble allies of the paramount rulers personally tilled a sacred corn field. It is thus possible that the corn of the Hopewellian epoch was solely a product of similar sacred fields. Not only did it appear at approximately the same time that this epoch of moundbuilding began, it also began to disappear from sites around A.D. 400, at roughly the same time that this epoch and its moundbuilding style came to an end. And it did not reappear in the valleys of the Ohio and Mississippi until about A.D. 700 or 800, after the third epoch of moundbuilding had begun.[9]

Food Supplies

Hunting, fishing, and gathering from the wild remained a significant way of obtaining food during the second moundbuilding epoch, but there is growing evidence that by 200 B.C. people throughout the region were cultivating local plants in order to increase their supply of edible seeds. Indeed, the seeds of sunflower and marsh elder undergo a dramatic transformation in the centuries between 200 B.C. and A.D. 400, which suggests not only that they were domesticated, but that people were engaged in the selective propagation of those plants that possessed the most desirable characteristics.

Since the people of this second moundbuilding epoch did know how to grow corn, one has to conclude that their continued reliance upon indigenous food plants was a matter of choice. And because they lived within such a rich forest environment, their choice, evidently, did not impose any hardship upon them. A team of archaeologists carried out a study in which they compared human bones from this epoch with those from later times when people were dependent upon corn, and their findings strongly suggest that people in the former period ate a more nutritious diet than those from the latter.[10]

High-Altitude Trails and a North–South Exchange

During the Hopewellian Period one of the most important relationships within the exchange network seems to have been a north–south connection between southern Ohio and the Copena site on the Tennessee River in northern Alabama, some 350 air miles southwest of Ohio. (Archaeologists gave this southern site its name "Copena," a combination of copper and galena, because of the unusual quantities of these northern minerals found there.) Although the roots of the Copena society were local, and its culture appears to be largely the result of an integration of secular and ceremonial practices from surrounding groups, its linkage to the Hopewellian centers is apparent both in artifact styles and mortuary practice.

Due to their southern location the Copena sites were in an excellent position to serve as collection points for southern products, especially those that came from two locations near the Gulf of Mexico, one in southwestern Alabama (the Mobile area) and one in the Chattahoochee Valley area of southwestern Georgia. Marine shells, marine turtle shells, sharks' and alligators' teeth, and barracuda jaws were brought there. Thus this linkage provided sites in Ohio with southern marine products and it provided Alabama sites with northern mineral products.

Ceremonialism flourished at the Copena center, where there are some fifty burial mounds. From this epoch, sites with the highest concentrations of galena are those in Ohio and the Copena sites in northern Alabama, where, so far, 450 kilograms of galena have been uncovered. Apparently the ore first moved down the Mississippi and up the Ohio River to the Ohio centers, and then moved south to Copena. An analysis of its trace elements indicates that it came from Upper Mississippi Valley deposits, located where Wisconsin, Illinois, and Iowa meet. These deposits are on the same riverine route that delivered copper from Lake Superior to more southern locales, so it is not surprising that large quantities of both ores were found at Copena. Archaeologists have found that most of the galena was consumed in burial ceremonies at Copena, and that smaller amounts were distributed from there to other sites in the south.

Given the importance of the relationship between southern Ohio and northern Alabama, it is quite possible that at least one of the major north–south roads during this period was an overland trail that ran above the fall line of the Appalachian Mountains. It is known from later periods that trails were more numerous above this line than below it, and it is unlikely that these high-altitude trails were used for hunting since they are far above the habitat of major game animals. If travelers used them, they would have avoided difficult river-crossings and swamps.[11]

Ceremonial Networks

Much more so than in either the first or third moundbuilding epoch, the mounds of the second, Hopewellian, epoch contain burials. In the Late Archaic Period, elite burials were already becoming elaborate, and by the time that Hopewellian culture spread throughout the moundbuilding region, they had become spectacular. The honored dead were sent off with an amazing array of goods, which included both great stashes of raw materials and finely finished pieces. (It is possible that the ceremonies associated with these mounds took place during various kinds of events and not just burials. Nevertheless, because burials leave behind such a good archaeological record, much of what is known about the Hopewellian networks does concern them.)

By 200 B.C., sites throughout the moundbuilding region display clear evidence that something more than highly valued strategic goods and ceremonial objects were being exchanged. Clearly there was also an exchange of ideas, a cultural dialogue of considerable proportions. Since the mounds were designed in similar ways, and more or less the same materials and goods are found in all parts of the region, and these goods appear to have been used in more or less the same ways and within the same context, archaeologists believe that after 200 B.C., all parts of the moundbuilding region participated in similar ceremonies and endowed certain objects and rituals with similar symbolic meanings. To various degrees, they all shared a similar world view. And since this world view called for ceremonies that required materials that could not be produced locally and had to be imported from other parts of the region, it encouraged the production and exchange of materials and finely crafted artifacts throughout the region.

Because there is so much similarity in the mounds and in the objects found at the mound sites, archaeologists continue to apply the single label "Hopewellian" not only to the Hopewell sites in Ohio but to sites throughout the moundbuilding region. Indeed, because of the material and cultural continuities some researchers once believed that an Ohioan center ruled over a great Eastern North American empire in more or less the same manner that, contemporaneously, Rome ruled the Mediterranean. However, as the archaeological evidence began to mount, it became clear that the various societies that participated in the ceremonial network remained quite distinct and that each retained its own local ways. It also appears that many of the Hopewellian-style goods were locally produced.[12] This suggests that Hopewellian ceremonies were established on top of local ceremonies and customs and not in place of them and that the Ohioan centers did not control the territories of those who participated in the ceremonies. Local cultures were not abandoned; they retained their vitality, and once the Hopewellian networks ceased to function, local identities and local traditions reemerged.

The Decline

The Hopewellian centers flourished for some 500 years, but sometime between A.D. 300 and 400 they began to decline, and so did mound-building, ceremonialism, and long-distance trading networks. Corn cultivation, too, was abandoned at about the same time. By A.D. 550, the Hopewellian phenomenon had disappeared completely. It has been suggested that the demise of corn cultivation due to climatic change may have been one of the causes of the decline. After A.D. 300, the weather might have become too cold and moist for tropical flint corn, which prefers a relatively dry climate with a moderately long growing season. However, at the present time there is little knowledge of climatic patterns in the eastern portion of the United States, and thus it is impossible to say what climatic changes occurred at this time.[13]

Furthermore, it seems unlikely that a decline in corn cultivation could cause the demise of the ceremonial centers. The peoples of this epoch were not dependent upon corn for their food supply. The other items associated with the Hopewellian networks—shells, mica, stones, ores, and so forth—would have been impervious to the weather, but they too disappeared along with the corn and the mounds. Indeed, if corn was used primarily as a ceremonial material, as suggested earlier, the demise of the ceremonies would explain the disappearance of the corn.

Another cause suggested for the demise of the Hopewellian networks involves a decline in the exchange of northern copper for southern coastal shells. It is definitely known that by the end of this epoch, peoples in the Southeast had discovered and begun to exploit local copper deposits. In the Appalachian Mountains from Virginia to Georgia, but especially near Ducktown, Tennessee, and in northwestern North Carolina, there were copper deposits which could be exploited with available technologies. When the Hopewellian networks were flourishing, small amounts of this southern copper were present in southeastern sites, but the majority of the copper in these sites came from the North, especially from Upper Michigan. However, after the Ohio centers began to decline, most of the copper in southeastern sites came from the Appalachian deposits. By about A.D. 500, all the copper in these sites was southern. Thus one possible explanation for the collapse of the Hopewellian ceremonial network is that once the southerners discovered copper deposits in their own region and began to develop their own copperworking traditions, they no longer were interested in exchanging Gulf Coast shells for northern copper. And, it has been suggested, once the principle reason for the exchange had been eliminated, the ceremonies were no longer held.[14]

This southern shift from northern to local sources of copper certainly is significant, but it is difficult to say whether it caused the collapse of the Hopewellian network or was a result of its collapse. It is possible to imagine the following scenario: a decline in mound-building and ceremonies accompanied a decline in long-distance trade; the trade decline caused a shortage of northern copper that, in turn, encouraged the peoples in the Southeast to increase their exploitation of Appalachian deposits; and they continued to rely upon these deposits during the subsequent moundbuilding epoch, even after a new ceremonial network had been created throughout the region.

One of the most interesting suggestions regarding the reason for the decline of the Hopewellian centers is that their ceremonial and exchange networks succumbed to endemic warfare brought about by the introduction of the bow and arrow. This weapon replaced the atlatl in the moundbuilding region of Eastern North America sometime between A.D. 300 and 550, at approximately the same time that Hopewellian networks declined and moundbuilding moved from the valleys to the hilltops and bluffs. Atlatl weights disappear around A.D. 400, and by the end of the Hopewell Period, mound sites were no longer built in open valleys where they would be vulnerable to outside attack. Instead, elaborate earthworks were located on inaccessible hilltops, where they could be defended more easily. Furthermore, at a number of these hilltop locations there is evidence of fires and massacres. By A.D. 600, the transition from the atlatl to the bow and arrow was complete.[15]

The introduction of the bow and arrow could have temporarily altered the balance of power and contributed to an increase in the frequency and the intensity of warfare. If it did, such warfare would have created disruptions along the exchange routes. And if the Hopewellian centers were unable to meet this challenge, their apparent weakness would have damaged the exchange networks and made it difficult to hold the ceremonies. Their weakness would also have cast doubt upon the legitimacy of the centers and the efficacy of their ceremonies.

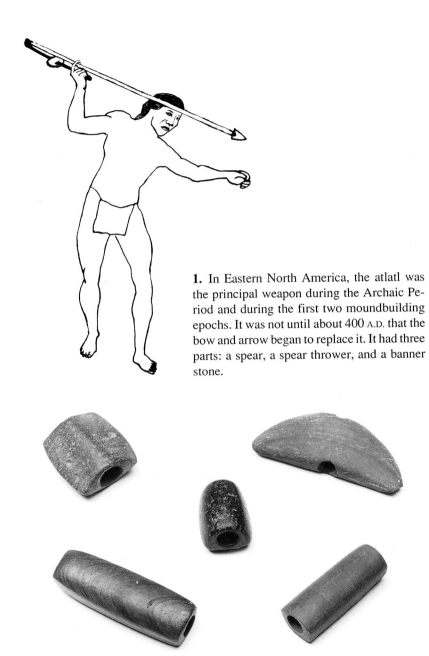

1. In Eastern North America, the atlatl was the principal weapon during the Archaic Period and during the first two moundbuilding epochs. It was not until about 400 A.D. that the bow and arrow began to replace it. It had three parts: a spear, a spear thrower, and a banner stone.

2. Banner stones were stones with holes drilled through them so that they could be slipped over the throwing stick of an atlatl. Presumably the weight of the stone added to the power behind each throw of the spear. Many banner stones were beautifully shaped and polished. (Courtesy, Frank H. McClung Museum, University of Tennessee.)

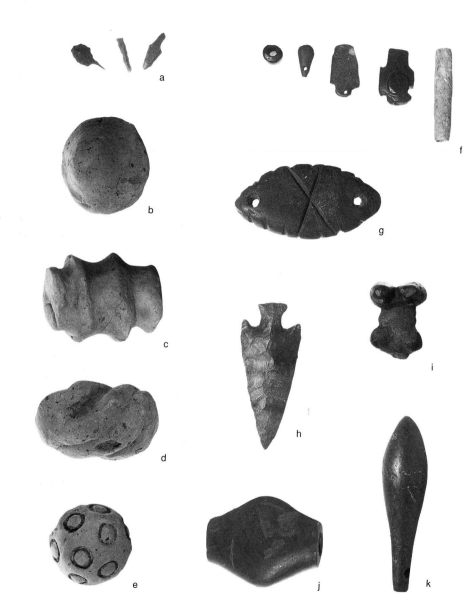

3. These objects were characteristic of the Poverty Point cultural area: *a,* microflints, possibly used as drills; *b-e,* clay cooking balls; *f,* stone beads and pendants; *g,* stone gorget (ornament on a necklace worn over the throat); *h,* stone projectile point; *i,* clay female torso; *j,* banner stone; *k,* plummet. (Courtesy, State of Louisiana, Division of Archaeology.)

4. This charming rendition of a locust is a red jasper bead about 2.25 inches long. A product of the Poverty Point culture, it is about three thousand years old. (Courtesy, Thomas Gilcrease Museum, Tulsa, Oklahoma.)

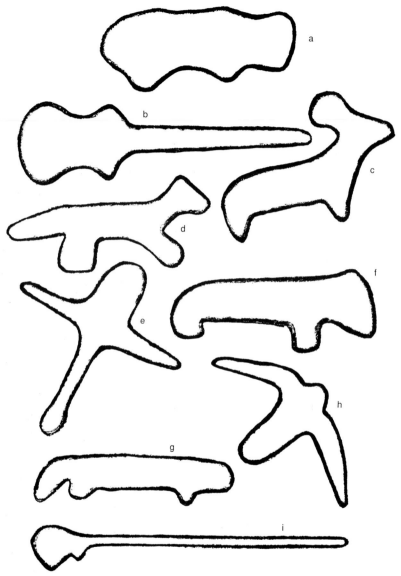

5. Effigy mounds were earthenworks made in the shape of animals. Most were only a few feet tall but more than one hundred feet in length. They are most typical of the Adena-Hopewell Period (ca. 500 B.C. to A.D. 500). The largest concentration of effigy mounds appears to have been in the southern half of Wisconsin where over 100 have been identified. The above shapes have been identified as: *a,* buffalo; *b,* turtle; *c,* deer; *d,* canine; *e,* bird; *f,* bear; *g,* beaver; *h,* bird; and *i,* panther. (Rowe, 1956: 70–71).

6. The Great Serpent Mound, which belongs to the Adena Period, is on the Ohio Brush River near Peebles, Ohio. If the snake could be stretched out to its full length, it would be 1,300 feet long. (Courtesy, Ohio Historical Society, Columbus.)

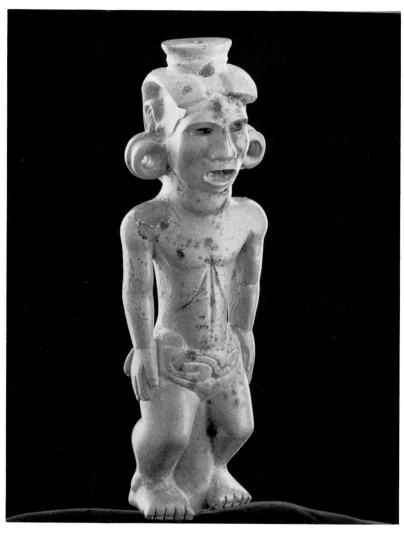

7. The male figure carved on this tubular Adena pipe wears earspools through his earlobes and a breechcloth bearing a serpent motif. (Courtesy, Ohio Historical Society, Columbus.)

8. Traces of pigment on Adena stone tablets suggest that they may have been used to stamp designs onto flat surfaces such as leather, bark, or various woven goods. The design on this one is a bird. (Courtesy, Ohio Historical Society, Columbus.)

9. This clay figurine depicting a mother and child was found in a Hopewellian burial mound in Illinois. (Courtesy, Milwaukee Public Museum.)

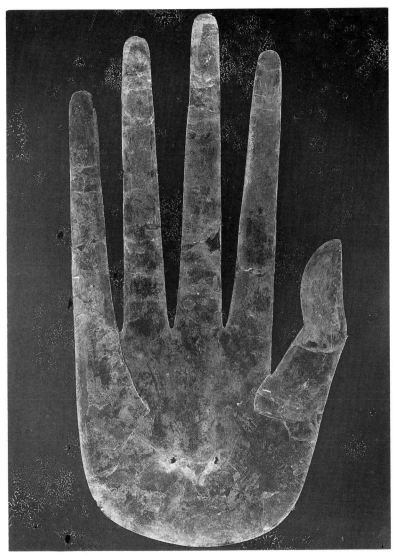

10. During the Hopewellian Period, thin sheets of mica (which came from the southern reaches of the Appalachian Mountains) were used to make cutout designs of various kinds. This hand-shaped cutout was found in Ohio. (Courtesy, Ohio Historical Society, Columbus.)

11. This stone platform pipe from the Hopewell Period was found in Illinois. The beaver's eyes are made from river pearls, and his teeth are made of bone. (Courtesy, Thomas Gilcrease Museum, Tulsa, Oklahoma.)

12. The bird portrayed on this stone platform pipe has been identified as a falcon. It was found in an Ohio Hopewell site. (Courtesy, Ohio Historical Society, Columbus.)

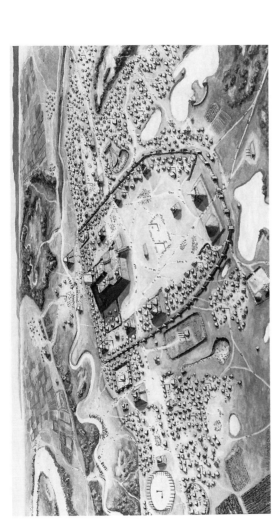

13. This painting by William Iseminger shows what "downtown" Cahokia might have looked like at its peak around A.D. 1200. It is based upon the archaeological work that has been done at the site. The tall roof of the Great Sun's abode is visible atop the palace mound, and similar but smaller structures can be seen on top of other smaller platform mounds. The latter may have been the residences of noble lineages allied to the Great Sun, or Honored Persons. The rectangular field, marked by two poles and located in the middle of the plaza, is a ball court. Outside the palisaded area, the rooftops of hundreds of small dwellings, the homes of commoners, are visible. Woodhenge, the solar horizon calendar, is on the left side of the painting. (Courtesy, Cahokia Mounts Historic Site.)

14. A recent photograph of Cahokia's palace mound, sometimes referred to as Monks' Mound. (Courtesy, Cahokia Mounts Historic Site.)

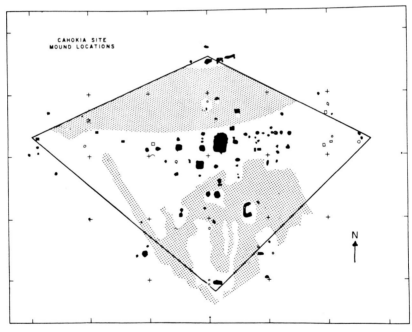

15. Over one hundred mounds once surrounded Cahokia's palace mound. If one draws lines between those that are located farthest east, south, west, and north, a diamond-shaped figure results. The area of the diamond is approximately six square miles. The shading indicates land that is below the 127 meter above sea level contour. (Abbreviated version of Fig. 73. p. 127, in Michael L. Gregg, "A Population Estimate for Cahokia," *Perspectives in Cahokia Archaeology*, Bulletin 10, 1975. Courtesy, Illinois Archaeological Survey, University of Illinois.)

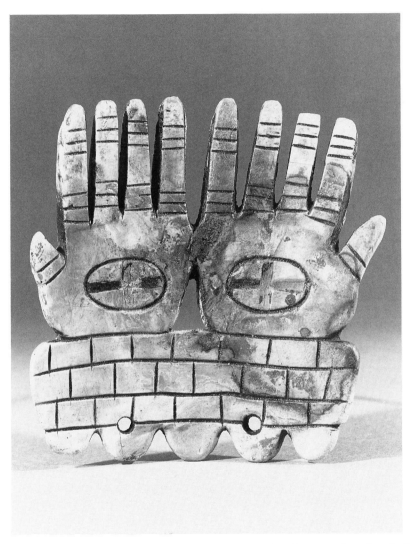

16. This pendant, about 3 1/3 inches high, is a carved and engraved marine shell cutout. It was found at Spiro, Oklahoma, and has been dated 1200–1350. (Courtesy, Thomas Gilcrease Museum, Tulsa, Oklahoma.)

17. This bird-costumed dancer was engraved on a Mississippian Period conch shell cup found at Spiro, Oklahoma. The rattle-shaped object on the dancer's necklace is a columella, a column-shaped part of the conch shell. (Courtesy, Museum of the American Indian, Heye Foundation.)

18. During the Mississippian Period, some of the finest copper repousse work was done at the Etowah center in northwestern Georgia. In this drawing of an Etowah piece, the dancer appears to be a warrior, with a mace in his right hand and a trophy head in his left. (Courtesy, University of Tennessee Press.)

19. This Mississippian piece, an 18-inch-tall sandstone figure, was found near Nashville, Tennessee. (Courtesy, Frank H. McClung Museum, University of Tennessee.)

20. The markings on the faces engraved on this piece of shell are those of the falcon. The circle represents the earth, and the lines radiating from the central face represent the four cardinal directions. (Courtesy, Museum of the American Indian, Heye Foundation.)

21. The water spider, whose image is portrayed on this engraved marine shell gorget, played an important role in Cherokee mythology. When animals first came to live on this earth, there was no fire to be had, and everyone was cold. Then lightning set fire to a sycamore tree located on an island, but none of the animals could figure out how to take away a glowing coal. Only the water spider knew what to do. She spun a thread from her body, wove the thread into a bowl, and attached it to her back. She swam to the island, placed a small ember in the bowl, and returned. Thus it was the water spider who brought the gift of fire to the creatures of this world. This gorget was found in Hamilton County, in eastern Tennessee, in a site dated to the latter part of the Mississippian Period. (Courtesy, Frank H. McClung Museum, University of Tennessee.)

22. This beaker (between 9 and 10 inches tall) was found at Cahokia. The scrollwork, which was etched on after the clay was fired, differs from that on local ceramics, and so it is thought to be an import. (Courtesy, Cahokia Mounds State Historic Site.)

23. Within the moundbuilding region, the eagle was a symbol of peace. This eagle, which is about 26 inches high, was carved on the top of a charnel house post sometime between A.D. 500 and 1000. It was found at the Fort Center site, west of Lake Okeechobee, Florida. (Courtesy, Florida Museum of Natural History, University of Florida.)

24. This notched hoe blade would have been bound to a wooden stick with leather thongs and a natural glue. After about A.D. 1000, such stone hoe blades can be found in the Mississippi Valley from Wisconsin to Tennessee. It appears that Cahokia artisans produced hoes in quantity, using imported chert blanks, most of which came from the Mill Creek site, about 100 miles southeast of Cahokia. (Courtesy, Cahokia Mounds State Historic Site.)

25. During the Mississippian Period, these stones, which have convex sides and are about the size of a flattened grapefruit, were used to play a game called chunkey. A player rolled a stone and threw a spear, trying to land the spear at the spot where the stone would eventually stop. West of the Mississippi River, this game was still being played in the nineteenth century. (Courtesy, Illinois State Museum).)

26. This smoothly polished figurine (known to archaeologists as the Birger Figurine), shown front and back, is about 8 inches tall and was carved from a reddish brown bauxite stone. It was found in the American Bottom near Cahokia and has been dated to the period when Cahokia was at its peak, 1000–1250. The female figure is depicted kneeling on a coiled serpent. In her right hand she is holding a hoe, stroking or scratching the serpent's back. On the back of the figurine, the snake's body divides and becomes two gourd vines. The gourd, which was under cultivation near the beginning of the Late Archaic Period (ca 3000 to 500 B.C.), was one of the first domesticated plants in the moundbuilding region. Thus this figurine clearly associates fertility with women, agriculture, the serpent, scratching or stroking, and the hoe. (Fig. 3b, p. 6 and Fig. 41, p. 7, in Thomas E. Emerson, *Mississippian Stone Images in Illinois*, Circular No. 6, February 1982. Courtesy, Illinois Archaeological Survey, University of Illinois.)

27. This 5-inch-tall figurine (known as the Keller Figurine) was found quite near the Birger Figurine, in the American Bottom near Cahokia. It also has been dated to the period between A.D. 1100 and 1250. It depicts a kneeling female figure with her left hand on a cloud-shaped metate (grinding bowl) and her right hand about to grasp a mano (a pestle). In the Mississippian Period, grinding tools would be closely associated with corn, and thus it has been suggested that the figurine could be a representation of Corn Mother.

The Corn Mother myth, which is told by several Southeastern peoples, descendants of the Mississippians, describes a Garden of Eden in which Corn Mother provides for her family by secreting herself, rubbing or scratching her abdomen, and giving birth to corn. The human family is tossed out of Eden and forced to work hard in the fields to raise corn after naughty children stealthily follow Corn Mother to her retreat and giggle over the delivery.

This figurine also provides rare information about women's styles during the Mississippian Period. Her hair is long, below waist level, and is combed back behind her ears. She is topless and wears a short, wraparound skirt and leather moccasins that go above the ankles. Unlike the figurine of the woman with the gourd, this woman has had her forehead flattened. It was the custom of several peoples in various parts of the Eastern Woodlands to fasten a board to an infant's skull in order to achieve this effect. (Fig. 5c, p. 9, in Thomas E. Emerson, *Mississippian Stone Images in Illinois*, Circular No. 6, February 1982. Courtesy, Illinois Archaeological Survey, University of Illinois.)

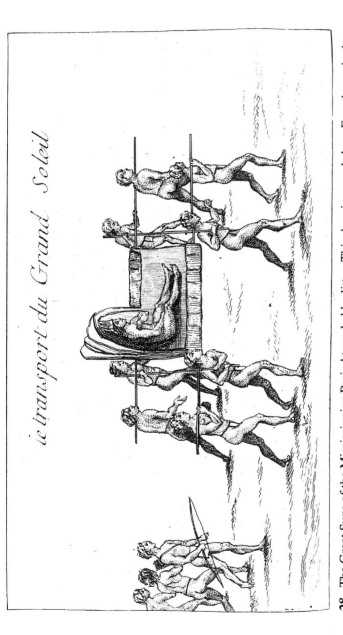

ie transport du Grand Soleil

28. The Great Suns of the Mississippian Period traveled by litter. This drawing, made by a Frenchman in the eighteenth century, shows the Great Sun of the Natchez (in northwestern Mississippi). Some burials at Cahokia contain several people, buried with litters, which suggests that not only the Great Suns, but other important persons may also have been permitted to travel in this way, at least on their journey to the grave. (Drawing reproduced from LePage Du Pratz, *Histoire de la Louisiane*, Paris, 1758. Courtesy, University of Georgia Libraries.)

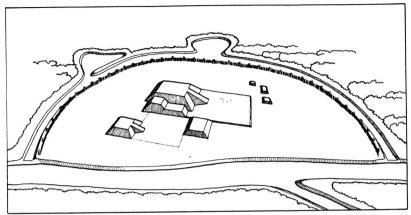

29. After A.D. 1250 and the decline of Cahokia, the Moundville site near Tuscaloosa, Alabama, another center within the Middle Mississippian subregion, continued to grow, and soon became one of the most important centers in the region. (P. 115 in William N. Morgan, *Prehistoric Architecture in the Eastern United States*, 1980. Courtesy, Massachusetts Institute of Technology Press.)

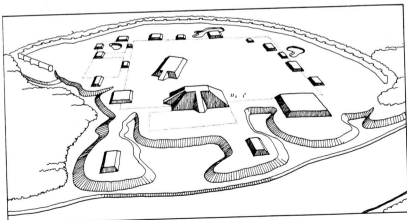

30. The Etowah site is located near Cartersville, Georgia, on what was once the frontier between the Southern Appalachian and Middle Mississippian subregions. Since many finely made objects have been uncovered at the site, it appears to have been a major crafts center, producing such items as copper repousse pieces and engraved shells. (Pp. xxxi, 117, in William N. Morgan, *Prehistoric Architecture in the Eastern United States*, 1980. Courtesy, Massachusetts Institute of Technology Press.)

31. Well over 60 feet high, the palace mound at Etowah was the second largest in the entire moundbuilding region (Morgan, 1980: xxx). In this photograph, members of the World History Association are about to begin their ascent to the top.

32. Although no cotton was grown or used within the moundbuilding region of Eastern North America prior to the arrival of Europeans and Africans, its peoples produced many kinds of textiles, using a variety of different fibers, furs, and feathers. This piece, a weaving made with plant fiber and rabbit hair, was found at Spiro, a Caddoan site in eastern Oklahoma. (Courtesy, Museum of the American Indian, Heye Foundation.)

33. During the Mississippian Period, the Caddoan subregion produced the most impressive ceramic wares. This small double bottle, little more than 6 inches tall, was found in western Arkansas. (Courtesy, Thomas Gilcrease Museum, Tulsa, Oklahoma.)

34. At the Davis site, on the Neches River near Alto, Texas, a typical Caddoan dwelling has been reconstructed. Although the interior is high enough to contain a loft, the doorway is low so people had to bend over to enter. (Courtesy, Loyd S. Swenson, University of Houston.)

35. In Indian Mounds Park, a city park in St. Paul, Minnesota, conical mounds line the bluff that overlooks both the Mississippi River and a large, flat, alluvial plain on the opposite shore.

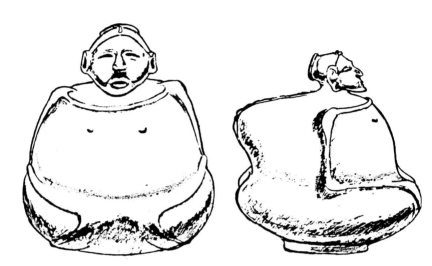

36. This ceramic pot, which is in the collection of the St. Louis Art Museum, accurately shows the vertebrae of a hunched-back person. After A.D. 1250, hunch-backed effigy pots can be found in many sites in the Middle Mississippian subregion. Some archaeologists believe that the manufacture of such pots is related to the presence of tuberculosis in at least some densely populated areas. (Drawing by Roger P. Levin.)

5 CAHOKIA AND OTHER MISSISSIPPIAN PERIOD CENTERS, THE THIRD MOUNDBUILDING EPOCH

Circa A.D. 700 to 1731

Today at Cahokia Mounds State Park in Collinsville, Illinois, one can stand atop the highest mound and see the skyline of St. Louis, Missouri, eight miles to the west on the opposite side of the Mississippi River. From about A.D. 900 to 1250, this site was the preeminent center of Eastern North America, the largest and presumably the most powerful center north of Mexico (Illustration 13). The 100-foot–high mound at its center is the world's largest earthwork, and in 1492 it was the third largest structure of any kind in the Western Hemisphere. (The two larger structures were—and are—in Mexico: the Temple of the Sun at Teotihuacan and the Temple of Quetzalcoatl at Cholula.) One thousand feet long and 700 feet wide, the site covers more than 15 acres. When Cahokia was at the peak of its development around A.D. 1200, whoever stood atop this mound could have counted more than 100 other mounds in the surrounding 5.8-square-mile site.[1] At least in terms of size, Cahokia was quite comparable to its Mexican contemporary, Tula, the capital of the Toltecs, which covered about 5.6 square miles.

The mounds at Cahokia belong to the third epoch of moundbuilding centers, what archaeologists call the Mississippian Period. Some would date its beginnings as early as A.D. 700, and the end of the epoch is often dated to 1550, close to forty years after Spanish expeditions to the region began.

Not all centers came to an end at the time of the invasions, however, and some continued to perform the Mississippian ceremonies long after the Spaniards had come and gone. The last may well have been the Natchez, whose center was destroyed by the French in 1731.

Cahokia Mounds State Park was named after the Cahokia Indians, the people who were living near the site in the early eighteenth century, when French traders and missionaries became the first Europeans to frequent the area. It is, however, unlikely that it was the Cahokias' ancestors who built the mounds. After 1492 and the arrival of Eastern Hemisphere people, North America underwent dramatic demographic and cultural changes, and by the eighteenth century not all the native peoples were in the same place that they had been in the precontact period. Archaeologists and historians are only now beginning to understand the relationship between precontact sites and postcontact peoples. Although it is by no means certain, oral traditions and fragments of historical evidence suggest that the rulers of Cahokia during the Mississippian Period belonged to the Dhegihan Sioux, a group that includes the Kansa, the Omaha, the Osage, the Ponca, and the Quapaw (who are also known as the Arkansa).[2]

The most characteristic earthwork of the third epoch is the platform mound (Illustration 14). Mounds of this variety have a rectangular base, and at the top are a series of flat tiers. They can be found by A.D. 500 in southwestern Georgia and in central Florida, and by about 700 they had spread to the Mississippi Valley and Cahokia.[3] Spanish accounts indicate that during the Mississippian Period paramount chiefs lived on top of these mounds in large and ornately decorated wooden buildings that some refer to as palaces and others as temples. In 1540, probably in what is now South Carolina, Hernando de Soto's expedition came upon such a building in a center that had been abandoned after the population was decimated by an epidemic. It would have been quite similar to the one atop Cahokia's platform mound, although much smaller, since this center was only about one-tenth the size of Cahokia. Since no one was there, the Spaniards went through the building. It was a single story but with a high ceiling. The roof was made of cane mats and covered with conch shells and freshwater pearls. Just inside the large doors were two rows of carved, wooden warriors. They held a variety of weapons—maces, batons, clubs, pikes, bows and arrows, and what look like wooden broadswords and battle-axes. There were also caches of valuables, including chests filled with freshwater pearls and bundles of furs. And in eight annexes there were large stores of leather shields and weapons.

Such platform mounds usually faced a large plaza, and smaller mounds were arrayed around it. Many of the latter were conical in shape.

Others were rectangular at the base, tapering off to a ridge at the top, rather like a loaf of bread. Platform mounds contain few burials. They were built in many stages, and it appears that whenever a ruler died, his palace on the mound was destroyed, and a new layer of earth was added. The new ruler's palace then was constructed atop the mound. Elite burials are most often found in the conical or ridge-topped mounds. This suggests that the height of a palace mound was a good measure of how long the chief's lineage had been paramount and that the number of conical and ridge-topped mounds indicated the number of lineages that had allied with the paramount chief. If this interpretation is correct, then any stranger approaching such a center could take one look around and easily judge the venerability of the ruling lineage as well as the number of its allies, which was a good measure of the military forces that it could mobilize.

The Center at Cahokia

The platform mound at Cahokia is located in the middle of a diamond-shaped site that covers about 2,000 acres (Illustration 15). It faces south, and once looked out over a large plaza. Some 400 acres around it, including the palace mound, the plaza, and some sixteen other mounds, were enclosed within a wooden palisade, a wall of large posts that was two miles in circumference and had a watch tower every seventy feet. The palace mound had its back up against the palisade's northern wall such that one could stand upon it and look south over the entire enclosure. (As the designers of China's imperial palaces well knew, such a south-facing position ensures that the sun's rays fall directly upon a structure throughout the day, and that all shadows are cast to the rear.)

At each of the diamond's points there was a mound marking one of the cardinal directions—north, south, east, or west. Outside the palisade but also within the diamond, archaeologists can now locate 3 additional plazas and another 77 mound sites, and they suspect that the number of mounds may once have totaled 120. Also within the diamond were a number of residential areas in which thatched-roof houses, usually rectangular in shape, were clustered at an average of several to an acre. Population estimates for the diamond-shaped site in the twelfth century range from 15,000 to 38,000.[4] If the 38,000 figure is accurate, Cahokia was comparable with the Toltec capital of Tula not only in size but also in numbers, since the Tula's population has been estimated to be 40,000.

About 1,000 yards west of Cahokia's platform mound, approximately 750 yards outside the palisade, was a structure now referred to as the "American Woodhenge," a precise circle some 410 feet in diameter and made up of 48 large posts. Four of these posts were positioned at the cardinal points, and the others were evenly spaced between them to form a complete circle. The structure appears to have been a calendrical device which enabled the supervisors of the ritual calendar to anticipate the coming of the solstices, the equinoxes, and other important dates. Their knowledge made it possible to make preparations and carry out the important ceremonies at just the right moment.

Raw materials found in some of the residential areas at Cahokia suggest that it had a number of artisan communities. People made pottery, wove baskets, fashioned shell beads, cut thin sheets of copper into ornaments, stitched leather clothing, and turned stones into tools. (The shell, copper, and many types of stone must have been imported from distant places since they cannot be found nearby.) It is quite likely that wooden tools and utensils were also produced but have not survived in the acidic soils of the area. Long-distance traders may have congregated there, and some of the neighborhoods appear to have been the homes of people who farmed, fished, and hunted nearby.

Art of the Mississippian Epoch

Like the mound sites, the art of the Mississippian Epoch is also distinct, although there clearly is some continuity in motifs from earlier epochs. One still sees, for example, the outline of the human hand and abstracted snakes and birds. Among the typically Mississippian subjects are dancers in elaborate bird costumes, and men and women in kneeling positions, carved in stone or in cedar which was then overlaid with copper sheeting. There are numerous images of warriors and hunters, represented either by a profile of the head or a combination of the profiled head with a frontal view of the body. Faces often have what look like tears running from the eyes, a representation of the hunter's face paint. (See Illustrations 16 through 22.) (The tear-like design resembles the markings on a hawk's eyes, a bird associated both with hunting and warring skills. The eagle, on the other hand, was associated with peace.)

Wooden carvings, mostly from Florida and Oklahoma, are among the most beautiful and expressive pieces from this era. One of the most poignant is an eagle, with its head bowed, carved atop a charnel house post (Illustration 23). (Some archaeologists do not consider this piece to be truly Mississippian, even though it is dated to the period A.D. 500 to 1000 and was found at Fort Center, west of Lake Okeechobee, a site that has a platform mound from the same period. They believe this Florida site to be too early and too atypical to be considered Mississippian.) Another Florida carving (which because of its relatively late date *is* considered to be Mississippian) is an elongated image of a cat sitting on its haunches. Found at Key Marco, a reproduction of it now graces a U.S. postage stamp.

Most of the Oklahoma carvings are from Spiro Mound on the Arkansas River near the Oklahoma–Arkansas border. This site has proved to be a veritable treasure trove of art and artifacts. That so many wood carvings survived at Spiro may be due to the fact that they were made of cedar and gilded with copper. Kneeling human figures, face masks (inlaid with pieces of shell), and a highly realistic turtle demonstrate the skill of the carvers. Giant-size marine shells and large quantities of copper repousse work(relief patterns made by hammering or pressing on the reverse side of a surface) have also been found. This rich site is, unfortunately, one of the most abused in the country. From 1933 to 1935 it was leased to commercial diggers, who plundered the main mound and upon their departure set off an explosion inside it in order to block access to any artifacts that they were forced to leave behind.

Some of the designs from the third epoch appear to be cosmographic symbols. Circles with crosses inside them were common, and often some motif—a geometric design such as a cross or a realistic image such as a frontal view of a hunter's face or a side view of a bird's beak—would be repeated within the circle four times, indicating the cardinal directions laid upon the earth (Illustration 20). Some of the circles have a zigzag design around them and thus appear to represent the sun as well as the earthly realm. The sun and the human eyeball seem to have been closely associated in the symbolic world of the Mississippians. The Choctaws, a people whose ancestors were Mississippians, have a tradition that the sun was a great blazing eye that watched over them, and a common Mississippian motif is a human eye with a prominent eyeball. Another, more abstracted version of this motif is a diamond-shaped eye with a large sphere in the middle. Cahokia's diamond-shaped site, the only one in the moundbuilding region, may have been related to this image. If so, the positioning of the Great Sun in its middle would have identified this ruler with the great blazing eye overhead. The Cherokees, another people descended from Mississippians, associate the sun with sacred fire and still, when laying a ceremonial fire, place the wood so that it forms various patterns similar to those that adorn Mississippian objects. (For example, some of the patterns used to lay a fire represent the sun, the earth, and the four cardinal directions.)[5]

Corn, Beans, and Salt

After the Hopewellian networks collapsed, corn disappeared from the moundbuilding region, but it reappeared several hundred years later, when the third moundbuilding epoch got underway. By A.D. 800 maize agriculture was firmly established in the region then emerging as Mississippian, and between 800 and 1000 its people became dependent upon corn as a mainstay of their diet. It was also after 800 that eastern flint corn, a South American or Mesoamerican variety, arrived in Eastern North America.[6] The tropical flint corn grown during the Hopewellian Period prefers a dry and warm climate. Eastern flint corn, on the other hand, is much hardier and does well in moist and cool climates. This new variety spread through the Eastern Woodlands between 800 and 1000, and indeed spread beyond the Woodlands where tropical flint corn had been found during the Hopewellian Period. It followed the Missouri River and its tributaries out onto the Great Plains, and to the east it spread over the Appalachians Mountains all the way to the Atlantic coast. By 1200 the old tropical flint corn had almost disappeared from the Eastern Woodlands. It was also during this third epoch that moundbuilding centers, in close association with the corn, spread out of the Woodlands for the first time.

At about the same time that the new corn appeared, so did fast growing beans domesticated in Mexico. (Some of these beans ripen within ten weeks.) These Mesoamerican beans come in many varieties, including kidney, navy, pinto, snap, and pole beans. It was common practice to grow them in corn fields and let them climb up the corn stalks.[7] (In those places where meat is seldom eaten, it is important to eat both corn and beans, for corn lacks lysine acid, one of the amino acids essential for protein production. Although Mississippian peoples did combine corn and beans, this was not necessary from a nutritional point of view since they were not vegetarians, and fish and game were plentiful.) Although the people within Cahokia's realm continued to fish and hunt for meat and hides and to gather or cultivate various local plants, corn displaced many of the indigenous seed crops upon which people previously had depended.

It was also during the Mississippian Period, sometime around 900, that the production and exchange of salt became important activities, yet another indication that people were dependent upon domesticated crops for a significant part of their food supply. People who rely on hunting and gathering often do not need to add salt to their food, since they generally receive adequate amounts from their usual diet. The same is not true for people who rely upon domesticated plants such as corn. If they do not add salt to their food, they can develop a potentially fatal salt deficiency.

Although there were a number of other methods that Mississippian peoples used to produce it, most of their salt was made from the waters of saline springs. These were concentrated in four areas: near the Red River in Louisiana, Arkansas, and Texas; along the Mississippi River near the confluence of the Missouri; along the Wabash River (now part of the border between Ohio and Indiana); and along the mid-reaches of the Ohio and up its southern tributaries into Kentucky, Tennessee, and West Virginia. Peoples in these areas were the salt producers, and others had to trade with them in order to acquire this necessity.[8]

Technologies and Other Developments

Archaeological finds indicate that by the time of the Mississippian Period the bow and arrow had replaced the atlatl, and the stone hoe was in general use (Illustration 24). The chroniclers of the Spanish expeditions describe many other tools and devices used by Mississippian peoples (some of which date back to previous epochs). In particular, the Spaniards found the canoes quite serviceable, as well as ropes and cables made of mulberry bark. They also made use of Mississippian rafts, causeways, and log bridges, some of which came complete with side rails.

Although many of the trade goods and ceremonial exchange items of this epoch were made from the same materials as those of the Hopewellian Period (mica, galena, copper, marine shells, and so forth), new sources for these materials seem to have developed. There are large quantities of chert arrowheads at Cahokia, some of them made from locally quarried stone, and some made from a black chert found in Arkansas and Oklahoma. Likewise the galena that in the Hopewellian Period had come mostly from the Upper Mississippi Valley now came mostly from the Potosi site in southern Missouri. And by this period copper was produced in southern Appalachia as well as in the Great Lakes region.

"Chunkey" stones first appear in sites from the Mississippian Period. These stones were shaped something like a pancake with hollowed out concave sides and were polished to a high sheen (Illustration 25). They are found throughout the moundbuilding region and were used to play a game called chunkey. In this game someone rolled one of the stones across a large field, and while it was still rolling the players threw spears at the point where they thought it would stop. The winner was the person whose spear landed closest to the point where the rolling stone fell.[9]

Villages and Towns

Another distinguishing feature of the Mississippian Period was the proliferation of villages and towns. A map that includes much of the moundbuilding region, which was probably drawn by a member of the de Soto expedition (1539–43), shows it to be dotted with palisaded towns. (See Map 8.) As the chroniclers of the expedition noted, the density of the villages and the abundance of food in many locales impressed the Spaniards. The following passages, which describe towns along the Mississippi and as far west as the Texas border, are only a few examples of many that could be cited:

> The Governor [de Soto] marched two days through the country of Casqui, before coming to the town where the cacique [chief] was, the greater part of the way lying through fields thickly set with great towns, two or three of them to be seen from one. . . .
> On Wednesday, the nineteenth day of June [1541], the Governor entered Pacaha, and took quarters in the town where the cacique was accustomed to reside. It was enclosed and very large. In the towers and palisades were many loopholes. There was much dried maize, and the new was in great quantity throughout the fields. At the distance of half a league to a league off were large towns, all of them surrounded by stockades. . . .
> About forty leagues from Quiguate stood Coligoa, at the foot of a mountain, in the vale of a river of medium size, like the Caya, a stream

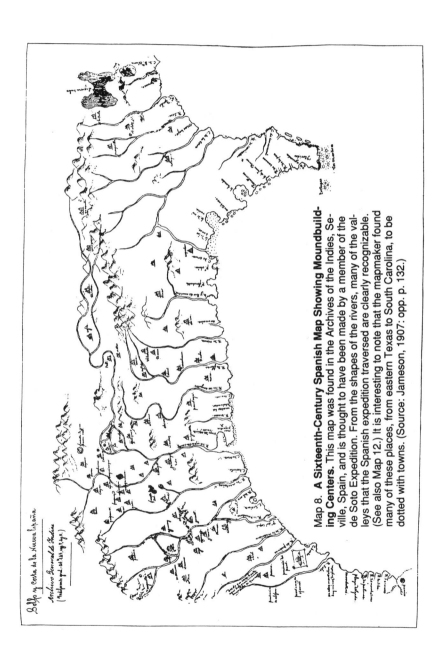

Map 8. **A Sixteenth-Century Spanish Map Showing Moundbuilding Centers.** This map was found in the Archives of the Indies, Seville, Spain, and is thought to have been made by a member of the de Soto Expedition. From the shapes of the rivers, many of the valleys that the Spanish expedition traversed are clearly recognizable. (See also Map 12.) It is interesting to note that the mapmaker found many of these places, from eastern Texas to South Carolina, to be dotted with towns. (Source: Jameson, 1907: opp. p. 132.)

that passes through Estremadura [Spain]. The soil was rich, yielding maize in such profusion that the old was thrown out of store to make room for the new grain. Beans and pumpkins were likewise in great plenty; both were larger and better than those of Spain: the pumpkins, when roasted, have nearly the taste of chestnuts. . . .

The following day, Wednesday, the twenty-ninth of March [1542], the Governor arrived at Nilco, making his quarters, and those of his people, in the town of the cacique, which was in an open field, that for a quarter of a league over was all inhabited; and at the distance of from half a league to a league off were many other large towns, in which was a good quantity of maize, beans, walnuts, and dried plums [persimmons]. . . .

At dawn at the sight of the town [Quigaltam], they came upon a scout, who, directly he saw the Christians, set up loud yells, and fled to carry the news to those in the place. . . . The ground was open field; the part of it covered by the houses, which might be a quarter of a league in extent, contained five or six thousand souls. . . .

The towns [the Spaniards] had burned in Naguatex, of which they had repented, they found already rebuilt, and the houses full of maize. That country is populous and abundant.[10]

Cahokia's Strategic Location

Although there were numerous large and important centers within the moundbuilding region during this third moundbuilding epoch, none compared with Cahokia. A few statistics should suffice to indicate its relative position. Ninety-two mounds have been located at Cahokia and there may have been as many as 120 at the site, whereas Mound-ville in Alabama, the second largest site, had 20, and Etowah in Georgia, the third largest site, once had 6. The volume in cubic yards of Cahokia's palace mound was about 804,608. It was thus five times larger than the region's second largest mound (159,331 cubic yards, at Etowah) and five-and-a-half times the size of the region's third largest mound (146,496 cubic yards, at Moundville).[11]

Why Cahokia grew so large, even in comparison with other centers of its time, was certainly related to its location. It sat at the conjunction of a number of very different ecological zones, and thus it could draw upon the resources provided by a wide variety of plants, animals, minerals, shells, and stones peculiar to each of the various zones. To its north was a marshy lowland and beyond that, the Great Lakes region.

To its southwest were the Ozark Mountains, and to its southeast was a zone of southern hardwood forests. Beyond these forests were the Appalachian Mountains. And to its south were the warm and sandy lands of the Gulf Coast.[12]

To its west were the Great Plains, immense grasslands where great buffalo herds grazed. Although there were farmers along some of the rivers that crossed the Plains, the majority of its peoples did not farm and depended upon hunting and gathering for their livelihood. And they sometimes traded their tanned buffalo hides for various Mississippian products. The villagers that de Soto met were well aware of the differences between themselves and the Plains peoples with whom they traded, and they seemed to think that the way of life of the Plains peoples needed some explanation. Some told de Soto that the weather was too cold on the Plains to farm, and thus it was thinly inhabited. Others said that the Plains people did not farm because there were so many buffalo that they would get into the fields and eat up all the crops.[13] More likely reasons are that the rains are less reliable on the Plains, and except along the rivers where alluvial soils are available, most of the soil is difficult to work without a plow.

Cahokia's location on the Mississippi meant that it was in a good position to facilitate north–south exchanges. But it may have been of equal importance that it was located just south of the mouth of the Missouri River, and not too far north of the mouth of the Ohio and its tributary, the Tennessee. It was thus in an excellent position to facilitate east–west exchanges. Given the significance of Rocky Mountain stones as raw materials for knives and arrowheads, Cahokia's access to goods coming down the Missouri River may have been a significant element in its success. That it was during the Mississippian Period that moundbuilding centers and corn cultivation first spread along this river beyond the woodlands and out onto the Great Plains also suggests the increased importance of the Missouri.

The American Bottom

Perhaps the most important factor in Cahokia's success was that it was located in the middle of the American Bottom, one of the finest agricultural sites in the Woodlands. A "bottom," in the local parlance, is a low-lying area, usually along the course of a waterway, and bottom soils are usually river-deposited sandy loams. Because they are exceedingly fertile and light (a characteristic that facilitates root development), these are choice soils, and the Mississippian peoples generally confined their farming to such alluvial deposits, since they could be easily worked with hoes.

The American Bottom, some 125 square miles in size, was a gift of the Missouri River. *Missouri* is an Indian word meaning "Big Muddy," and the river was so called because in its long journey across the prairies and plains from Montana to the western border of Illinois, it picks up large amounts of silt. The bluff that forms the eastern rim of the Mississippi Valley stays the waters of the Missouri as they pour into the Mississippi, and over the millennia, as the river meandered over the land in front of the bluff, it left behind the silt that created the American Bottom. This deposit of sandy loam is about 120 air miles long, from Alton, Illinois, in the north to Chester, Illinois, in the south. At its northern tip the valley is fairly narrow, but below the point where the Missouri River joins the Mississippi, it spreads out such that it is about eleven miles across. The wide part of the valley is about twenty-five miles long, but in the Dupo, Illinois, area it narrows once again. (See Map 9.)

Cahokia was by far the largest population center in the American Bottom, but it was by no means the only one. The entire Bottom was densely populated. By A.D. 1000, within a twenty-five–mile radius of Cahokia, there were four other large centers. The Mitchell site is at the northern end of the valley, near the mouth of the Missouri. South of Cahokia where the valley narrows is the Pulcher site, and the remaining two were precisely where St. Louis and East St. Louis are today, one west of the river, and one east of the river. In addition four middle-sized centers and about fifty small farming villages have been located in the valley.[14]

Mississippian Society and the Great Suns

Burials at Cahokia and other centers suggest that Mississippian societies were divided into ranks or classes. Some of the elite burials were quite spectacular. In one Cahokian grave the bodies of six individuals were laid to rest along with large pieces of rolled sheet copper and mica, chunkey stones, and a large cache of arrowheads. Nearby was one man, buried alone upon a blanket made entirely of marine shell beads. This grave also contained the cedar posts of a litter.

Spanish and French accounts confirm what the archeological evidence

Map 9. **Recorded Sites of the American Bottom.** The largest single deposit of sandy loam in the Eastern Woodlands, this low-lying bottomland is 120 miles long and 11 miles across at its widest point. The thicker lines around the edges (the 500-foot contour) mark the bluffs that surround the bottom and have confined the meanderings of the river. The largest of the lakes shown is Horseshoe Lake, immediately northwest of Cahokia. The two second line communities that face each other across the Mississippi River are located where St. Louis and East St. Louis are today. (Abbreviated and reproduced with the permission of the Illinois Archaeological Survey, University of Illinois. Fig. 74, p. 128 in Michael L. Gregg, "A Population Estimate for Cahokia," *Perspectives in Cahokia Archaeology*, Bulletin 10, 1975.)

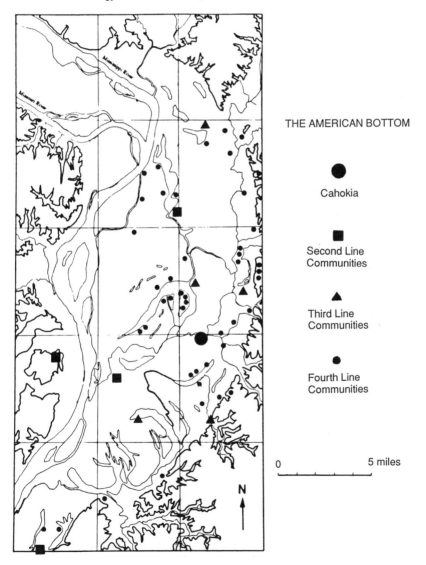

THE AMERICAN BOTTOM

Cahokia

Second Line
Communities

Third Line
Communities

Fourth Line
Communities

0   5 miles

N

Map 10. **Distribution of Galena at Mississippian Sites in Illinois.** Galena, a lead-sulphide ore often used as a white pigment, is an important marker of ceremonial activity. Thus the ceremonial preeminence of Cahokia is obvious from this map. The shaded areas mark the location of important sources of this mineral, the Upper Mississippi Valley (UMV) and Southeastern Missouri-Potosi Formation (SEM-II). (Reproduced with permission of the Illinois State Museum, Springfield, Fig. 12, p. 40 in John A. Walthall, *Galena and Aboriginal Trade in Eastern North America*, Scientific Papers Vol. XVII, 1981.)

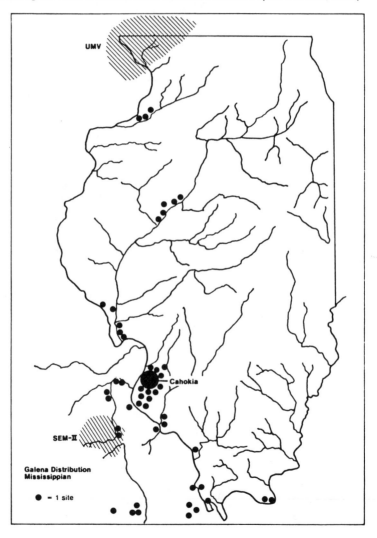

suggests: the existence of class stratification and paramount rulers during the Mississippian Period. Both describe rulers known as Great Suns and indicate that they were surrounded in life, as well as in their graves, by Mississippian luxuries. They were often attired in knee-length fur cloaks. One cloak, which was made out of marten skins and worn by a ruler in South Carolina, was judged by a Spaniard to be worth two thousand ducats (roughly $4,500) in Spain. In a place called Palisema, both the ceiling and the floor of the ruler's residence was covered with beautifully tanned deerskins which had been painted with multicolored designs. This would indicate that not all of the luxury is still apparent in the graves, since leather and fur, like many materials, do not survive in the acidic soils of the region.

Sixteenth-century Spanish accounts also tell us something about the political hierarchy. They describe a paramount chief in Florida, a class of notables who brought him tribute, and a class of "principal men." The rest of his subjects were referred to as commoners. Eighteenth-century French accounts of the Natchez, a people in western Mississippi, indicate that they were still ruled by a royal lineage that claimed descent from the sun. Royal succession followed a matrilineal descent system within which each "Great Sun" was replaced by a nephew, one of his sisters' sons. A class of nobles was allied with the Great Sun's lineage, and there was also a group known as Honored Peoples. The commoners were called "Stinkards." Some Native American peoples also had slaves, who were usually prisoners of war whom they had decided to keep. Apparently, these people were not thought of as part of the four-class structure.

Among the Natchez, the supremacy of the Great Sun was explained by a legend that described a man and a woman who descended to earth from the Upper World. They had come to govern humans and to teach them how to live better. The man, said to be the younger brother of the sun (believed to be female by some), commanded the people to build a temple. In this temple they placed a sacred, perpetual fire, a piece of the sun brought to earth. When the man died, he turned himself into stone so that he would not be corrupted by the earth.[15]

A number of sites, in Georgia and Tennessee, as well as in Illinois, have yielded male and female stone images. Two female figures, both of them kneeling, have been found at Cahokian sites. The first, the Birger sculpture, has her left hand on the head of a snake. The snake's body coils around her, and her right hand holds a hoe, with which she is scratching, or tilling, the back of the snake. Across her back is a vine, with what look like gourds or squash hanging from it (Illustration 26). The second woman, the Keller sculpture, has lost her right arm and hand, and only the left hand remains (Illustration 27). It is resting on a metate, a stone dish used to grind corn. Some have pointed out that the metate looks like a cloud, and have suggested that the vertical lines descending from it may represent rain. Others think the lines represent ears of corn stood on end. Both of these figures are clearly related to fertility and both seem to be related to elements of the Corn Mother myth, which was widespread among southeastern peoples. There are several versions of the myth, but all involve Corn Mother scratching some part of her body to give birth to corn.[16]

The Great Sun of the Natchez, whose duty it was to keep the sacred fire burning and to perform other rituals, had to be treated with great deference and had to be kept ritually pure. He was carried in a canopied litter (Illustration 28). Only certain people were allowed into his presence, and they had to follow elaborate procedures before approaching him. No one could see him eating nor even touch the vessels from which he ate. People from all the Natchez villages were obliged to bring him tribute, usually crops, and his head warriors personally tilled sacred corn fields on his behalf. His subjects were also obliged to lend him their labor for the construction of public works. In return, he was expected to be exceedingly generous and to redistribute this tribute to his subjects.

It is also apparent that Mississippian societies engaged in human sacrifice when a ruler or high-ranking noble died. There is no evidence of such a practice in the earlier moundbuilding epochs. It seems to have begun at Kolomoki (in Georgia), which was also an early site of the platform mound. Although the burials at the Cahokian center indicate more sacrificial activity than other sites, the practice seems to have been widespread throughout the region.[17] The Spaniards found out about it in 1542 when de Soto died from disease along the banks of the Mississippi. His men tried to keep his death a secret from the local people, but their ruler knew very well what had happened and arrived at the Spanish camp with two young men whom he offered as sacrificial victims. He explained "that it was the usage of the country, when any lord died, to kill some persons who should accompany and serve him on the way [to the afterlife], on which account they were brought."[18]

The French also learned. French chroniclers were present among the Natchez in 1725 when Tattooed-Serpent died. He was an honored war chief and the brother of the Great Sun. Those who sacrificed themselves at his funeral included two of his wives, one of his sisters, his first warrior, his healer, his head servant and speaker (whose wife accompanied him in death), his nurse, and a man who made war clubs. Some of the French were friendly with one of the wives and tried to dissuade her from participating. She replied:

> He [Tattooed-Serpent] is in the country of the spirits, and in two days I will go to join him and will tell him that I have seen your hearts shake at the sight of his dead body. Do not grieve. We will be friends for a much longer time in the country of the spirits than in this, because one does not die there again. It is always fine weather, one is never hungry, because nothing is wanting to live better than in this country. Men do not make war there anymore, because they make only one nation. I am going and leave my children without any father or mother. When you see them, Frenchmen, remember that you have loved their father and that you ought not to repulse the children of the one who has always been the true friend of the French.[19]

Ceremony at the Center

Although the nature of the relationship between Cahokia and other parts of the moundbuilding region is not yet understood, it is clear from the archaeological record that these relationships were significant. The mounds, the plazas, and the burials were quite similar throughout the region where Mississippian Period moundbuilding centers were located. An elaborate exchange network supplied the centers with the necessary ceremonial goods, most of which had to be imported. Given the disproportionate size of Cahokia and the disproportionate number of mounds, the unusual concentration of ceremonial and strategic materials (see Map 10, page 64), and the higher frequency of elite burials there, it seems likely that the Cahokia center enjoyed some sort of ceremonial prominence within the region that led to the concentration of noble people and valuable materials at the site.

Spanish accounts indicate that Mississippian peoples were familiar with the ceremonial display of paramount power. Centers may well have used these ceremonies to display their allies and thus their power, and it seems that one's place during the ceremonies revealed the significance of one's relationship to the center. The following passage, for example, demonstrates that after Spanish military capabilities became known, local rulers cared a great deal about the closeness of their relationship to the Spaniards and how it was displayed:

> The Governor [de Soto] made friendship between the chiefs of Casqui and Pacaha [in Arkansas], and placed them at the table that [they] should eat with him. They had a difficulty as to who should sit at his right hand, which the Governor quieted by telling them that among Christians the one seat was as good as the other.[20]

It is also clear from the accounts of de Soto's expedition that the creation of an alliance with a paramount power involved gifts given and alliances sealed by a marriage between the paramount ruler and a woman from the allied lineage.

> [The Chief of Casqui ordered] three barges to draw near, wherein was great quantity of fish, and loaves like bricks, made of the pulp of plums [persimmons], which de Soto receiving, gave him thanks and again entreated him to land. . . .
> The cacique of Casqui many times sent large presents of fish, shawls, and skins. . . .
> The Chief of Casqui came the next day, and after presenting many shawls, skins, and fish, he gave [de Soto] a daughter, saying that his greatest desire was to unite his blood with that of so great a lord as he was, begging that he would take her to wife. . . .
> [De Soto] rested in Pacaha forty days, during which time the two caciques made him presents of fish, shawls, and skins, in great quantity, each striving to outdo the other in the magnitude of the gifts. At the time of his departure, the chief of Pacaha bestowed on him two of his sisters, telling him that they were tokens of love, for his remembrance, to be his wives. The name of one was Macanoche, that of the other Mochila. They were symmetrical, tall, and full: Macanoche bore a pleasant expression; in her manners and features appeared the lady; the other was robust.[21]

De Soto and the Cacique of Quigaltam

By the spring of 1542, de Soto thought that he had mastered the system of alliance networks that characterized the moundbuilding region and began to claim that he, himself, was a Great Sun. When he had been powerful, local rulers came to him offering tribute, hoping to forge an alliance with him against their enemies. But by this time de Soto's ability to attract allies was withering away. Already he had lost half of his men and all but forty of his horses, and he was still losing men and horses at a steady pace. Furthermore, after his best interpreter died, de Soto no longer wanted to lead his army into unknown territory for fear that the expedition would get lost. He was then in what is now Arkansas, so he returned to the western bank of the Mississippi River with the intention of going back to Spanish bases in Cuba in order to get reinforcements and supplies.

Before he could leave, he had to find a town on the Mississippi River with abundant provisions where his men could spend the summer constructing seaworthy vessels to take them down the river and across the Gulf of Mexico to Cuba. The larger towns in Arkansas had now turned against him and were denying him their supplies so that he would be forced to leave their territories. He tried sending runners far afield saying that he was a "Child of the Sun . . . and whence he came all obeyed him, rendering him tribute." One of his messengers managed to go as far south as Quigaltam, on the eastern bank of the Mississippi River, in what is now northern Mississippi. (Some authorities believe that the Natchez, who lived in this location in the eighteenth century, were the descendants of the Quigaltam people.)

Although de Soto's attempt to manipulate the local system failed miserably, it did provoke a reply from the ruler of Quigaltam that is one of the most revealing statements ever made about Mississippian politics. Quigaltam had one of the largest and most thickly settled populations in the Mississippi Valley. A Spanish account from the sixteenth century indicates that its principal town had some 500 houses and that its paramount chief could mobilize some thirty or forty thousand warriors. Although this estimate of his forces may be an exaggeration, there is no doubt that he was a major power in the region between the Lower Mississippi Valley and the Gulf of Mexico and that he had no intention of submitting to de Soto's demands. He replied to de Soto as follows:

> As to what you say of your being the son of the Sun, if you will cause him to dry up the great river, I will believe you: as to the rest, it is not my custom to visit any one, but rather all, of whom I have ever

heard, have come to visit me, to serve and obey me, and pay me tribute, either voluntarily or by force. If you desire to see me, come where I am; if for peace, I will receive you with special good-will; if for war, I will await you in my town; but neither for you, nor for any man, will I set back one foot.[22]

A Chinese emperor could not have put it better.

Military Capabilities

Accounts of the Spanish expeditions make clear that control over highly valued and strategic materials distributed through ceremonial exchange was not the only mechanism by which Mississippian centers persuaded potential allies to participate in their ceremonies and bring them tribute. The centers were able and willing to back up their ritual powers with force. Even the Spaniards, with their gunpowder, iron weapons, and horses, had good reason to fear them. The description of a fleet of canoes "like a famous armada of galleys" referred to in chapter 1 is quoted below, along with other expressions of Spanish respect for the capabilities of Mississippian warriors:

> The next day the cacique [the paramount chief] arrived with two hundred canoes filled with men, having weapons. They were painted with ochre, wearing great bunches of white and other plumes of many colors, having feathered shields in their hands, with which they sheltered the oarsmen on either side, the warriors standing erect from bow to stern, holding bows and arrows. The barge in which the cacique came had an awning at the poop, under which he sate [sic]; and the like had the barges of the other chiefs; and there, from under the canopy, where the chief man was, the course was directed and orders issued to the rest. . . . These were fine-looking men, very large and well formed; and what with the awnings, the plumes, and the shields, the pennons, and the number of people in the fleet, it appeared like a famous armada of galleys.[23]

> If they fear an enemy they are awake the night long, each with a bow at his side and a dozen arrows. . . . The method they have of fighting, is bending low to the earth, and whilst shot at they move about, speaking and leaping from one point to another, thus avoiding the shafts of their enemies. So effectual is their maneuvering that they can receive very

little injury from crossbow or arquebus; they rather scoff at them; for these arms are of little value employed in open field, where the Indians move nimbly about. They are proper for defiles and in water; everywhere else the horse will best subdue, being what the natives universally dread.[24]

. . . Having told [de Soto] that he [the cacique of Casqui] would deliver into his hands the cacique of Pacaha, he went to Casqui, and ordered many canoes to ascend the river, while he should march by land, taking many warriors. [De Soto], with forty cavalry and sixty infantry, was conducted by him up stream; and the Indians who were in the canoes discovered the cacique of Pacaha on an islet between two arms of the river. Five Christians entered a canoe . . . to go in advance and see what number of people the cacique had with him. There were five or six thousand souls. . . .

Then the town where they were, as soon as the winter should set in, would become so surrounded by water, and isolated, that no one could travel from it by land farther than a league, or a league and a half, when the horses could no longer be used. Without them we were unable to contend, the Indians being so numerous; besides, man to man on foot, whether in the water or on dry ground, they were superior, being more skillful and active, and the conditions of the country more favorable to the practice of their warfare.[25]

When de Soto's expedition was making its exit down the Mississippi River and out into the Gulf of Mexico, the ruler of Quigaltam and his allies had no intention of letting the Spaniards get away with their remaining forces intact:

The next day a hundred canoes came together, having from sixty to seventy persons in them, those of the principal men having awnings, and themselves wearing white and colored plumes, for distinction. . . . Thence they all came down yelling, and approached the Spaniards with threats. [De Soto] sent Juan de Guzman, captain of foot, in the canoes, with twenty-five men in armor, to drive them out of the way. So soon as they were seen coming, the Indians, formed in two parts, remained quietly until they were come up with, when, closing, they took Juan de Guzman, and those who came ahead with him, in their midst, and, with great fury, closed hand to hand with them. Their canoes were larger than his, and many leaped into the water—some to support them, others to lay hold of the canoes of the Spaniards, to cause them to capsize, which was presently accomplished, the Christians falling into the water, and, by the weight of their armor, going to the bottom; or when one by swimming, or clinging to a canoe, could sustain himself, they with paddles and clubs, striking him on the head, would send him below.[26]

6 SUBREGIONS, OUTPOSTS, AND THE DECLINE OF CAHOKIA

At least six cultural subregions developed during the third, or Mississippian, moundbuilding epoch. (See Map 11.) Each subregion, to varying degrees, possessed noticeable continuities in customs and styles that clearly distinguish it from the others. Although there had been culturally distinct areas during the second, or Hopewellian, period, they were small in scope and much more numerous. Mississippian subregions were large, and generally encompassed significant portions of what would become several states. The Middle Mississippian subregion was at the center, and arrayed around it were the Southern Appalachian, Plaquemine, Caddoan, Oneota, and Fort Ancient.[1] One could also delineate an additional, seventh, subregion in Florida. The centers of these subregional cultures participated at some level in the Mississippian ceremonial, and while they did so, they were able to bring about an unprecedented degree of consolidation and cultural continuity within their own locales.

The Subregions

The largest of the cultural subregions was the Middle Mississippian. It included the Cahokian center and the Mississippi Valley from the mouth of the Illinois in the north to the mouths of the White and St. Francis rivers (in Arkansas) in the south. It also extended eastward along the lower Ohio River and along the Tennessee River and its tributaries all the way to North Carolina. It was, itself, a geographically diverse area with many different specialities, and, given its central location, it also could draw upon the specialties of all the other subregions.

Map 11. **The Moundbuilding Region During the Mississippian Period (ca. A.D. 700 to 1731).** This is an abbreviated version of a map prepared by the Museum of Anthropology, University of Michigan, and first published in James B. Griffin, "Eastern North American Archaeology: A Summary," *Science* 156:3772, 175–91 (14 April 1967). Although this map was drawn in 1967 and thus does not reflect all that has been learned since then, it still is one of the best available maps of the region. (Copyright 1967, by the American Association for the Advancement of Science.)

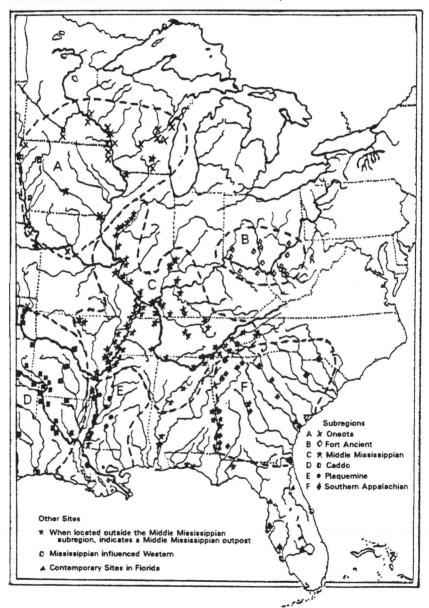

Subregions

A ⋇ Oneota
B ◇ Fort Ancient
C ✶ Middle Mississippian
D ◻ Caddo
E ● Plaquemine
F ◆ Southern Appalachian

Other Sites

✶ When located outside the Middle Mississippian
   subregion, indicates a Middle Mississippian outpost

◻ Mississippian influenced Western

▲ Contemporary Sites in Florida

The Middle Mississippian subregion also reached far south into what is now Alabama. It thus included the center at Moundville (Illustration 29), which is located about fourteen miles south of Tuscaloosa, on the Black Warrior River. After the decline of Cahokia around A.D. 1250, the Moundville center not only continued to flourish but grew to become the largest center in the region in the centuries immediately before the Spanish arrival. At its largest, it covered some 300 acres and had about twenty mounds.

Moundville was in a good position to amass shells coming from the Gulf Coast and to exchange them for northern products.[2] In this respect its role seems to have been similar to that of the Copena site in northern Alabama during the Hopewellian era. But in at least two other ways, Moundville differed from the earlier northern Alabama site. The Copena sites had been in the Tennessee River valley, whereas the Moundville site is south of the Mississippi drainage, almost halfway to the Gulf; the waters of the Black Warrior River flow eventually into Mobile Bay and the Gulf of Mexico. Moundville was also different from Copena in that it was located on a large deposit of alluvial soil that was ideal for farming, a difference that points to the significance of agriculture during this third epoch of moundbuilding.

The Southern Appalachian subregion included most of Georgia and South Carolina, and part of North Carolina. Its largest center was at Etowah, which is in northwestern Georgia near Cartersville. The center at Etowah (Illustrations 30 and 31), which once had six mounds, was the third largest in the entire moundbuilding region, and its palace mound was second in size only to the one at Cahokia. The site appears to have served as a gateway from the Middle Mississippian subregion into the Southern Appalachian, since it was located just outside the watershed of the Tennessee River, and almost on the boundary that separated these two subregions. It also had good connections to the Gulf, since it was on the Etowah River, whose waters eventually end up in the Gulf via Mobile Bay.

Both the South Carolina and Georgia coasts were within the zones where the three most desirable marine shells could be found, and Etowah became a collection point for these shells whence they were transported into the Middle Mississippian region. But the handicraft skills of its people may have been of more significance than any trade in unadorned shells. They etched intricate designs on the shells, turned out finely worked copper pieces, and carved appealing sculptures of sandstone. Appalachian copper deposits were nearby, and most of the copper pieces found in Mississippian sites in Georgia, Alabama, and Florida were made from ore that came from these southern deposits.[3]

Florida lay to the south of the Southern Appalachian subregion. Its beaches yielded up several varieties of valuable shells, and its peoples, especially those who lived in its southern half, were much involved with the sea and with nearby islands. Unlike other Mississippians, but quite like peoples in the Caribbean Islands, they cultivated the *Zamia* plant (a tuber) for food. They fished with nets, ropes, stakes, and elaborate traps, and they took their large dugout canoes onto the high seas where they used harpoons to take whales, sharks, sailfish, porpoises, seals, and sea turtles. The Calusa, with their double-hulled canoes, were able to go to the Bahamas and Cuba to trade, and they were also the people who attacked and did serious damage to Ponce de León's expeditions. They maintained their canoe routes to Cuba long after the Spaniards took the island, and were still visiting there in the eighteenth century.[4]

South of the Middle Mississippian subregion was the Plaquemine. This subregion was located in the Lower Mississippi Valley, and it covered much the same geographical area that the Poverty Point cultural area had covered about two thousand years previously. The presence of Middle Mississippian influence and Middle Mississippian peoples is apparent in the archaeological record, but what is most obvious are the strong continuities with earlier cultures in the Lower Mississippi Valley during both the Hopewellian and Poverty Point periods. For example, finely crafted and decorated clay objects, including pipes, pots, and small figurines and ornaments, have been found in Plaquemine sites, and both various aspects of their production and their distinctive style are reminiscent of objects produced in the area during earlier periods.

The Caddoan cultural subregion was located in the southwestern portion of the Mississippian realm, in southern Missouri, Arkansas, western Louisiana, and eastern Oklahoma and Texas. The de Soto expedition, which spent some time there, was impressed by the size of the population, the abundance of corn, and the technical capabilities its peoples displayed (Illustration 32). One of the expedition's chroniclers described an elaborate process by which Caddoan peoples collected and purified the salt found in sandbanks along some of the rivers, and the Spaniards also learned from them how to make complicated spring traps to catch rabbits. The subregion is well known for its pottery (Illustration 33), some of the finest made anywhere in the mound-building region. The Spaniards were duly impressed by the wares they saw in Arkansas and compared them to those of Estremoz and Montemor in Spain.[5]

Prior to the time that Cahokia flourished, just as the third epoch of moundbuilding centers was emerging, centers in the Caddoan region may have enjoyed preeminence. Between A.D. 700 and 900 the Plum Bayou site on the Arkansas River in central Arkansas was one of the largest centers in Eastern North America. It was located on a large silt-laden plain with oxbow lakes and had eighteen mounds, including a flat-topped platform mound, and a plaza. There was a proliferation of bow and arrow technology in this locale after 600 A.D., at about the same time that moundbuilding began at Plum Bayou, and its residents had good access to valuable stone deposits. The meat and fish supply was similar to that in the Lower Mississippi Valley, and residents ate considerable quantities of the starchy seeds of chenopodium, may-grass, and little barley and small amounts of corn. However, around 900, at the same time that Cahokia's prestige and power was consoli-dated, the Plum Bayou site was abandoned.[6]

Thereafter, two other sites in Caddoan country flourished: the Spiro, Oklahoma, site, where many fine artifacts have been unearthed, and the Davis Site on the Neches River near Alto, Texas. Both were lo-cated near the western boundary of the Eastern Woodlands and engaged in trade with the hunting and gathering peoples of the Plains. The Davis site was auspiciously located at the edge of the Piney Woods, which is also the edge of the Woodlands in Texas, and just north of the marshy Big Thicket. The earliest Caddoan settlers arrived at the site around A.D. 800, with bow and arrow already in hand. The only domesticated crop so far identified is eastern flint corn. There are two platform mounds and one conical burial mound at the site, which seems to have reached its peak around 1100. Pottery manufactured at the site was bone-tempered and made by the coil method. (When using this method, the potter first shapes a long, rope-like piece of clay that resembles a snake, and coils it round and round first to form the bottom of a vessel and then to build up its sides.) The people lived in tall thatched houses that were circular at the ground and rose to a point at the top, a design that has given rise to the term Caddo Gothic (Illustration 34). They varied in size from twenty-five to forty-five feet in diameter.[7]

To the north of Cahokia, in the vicinity of the Upper Mississippi, was the Oneota cultural subregion. It included northern Missouri, Iowa, most of Wisconsin, and a large part of southern Minnesota. It possessed many valuable and strategic ores, which were quarried and transported down the rivers. Its northern-most center (Illustration 35) was in the St. Paul–Minneapolis area,[8] which would have been a convenient collection point for ores coming from Lake Superior copper deposits. The Upper Mississippi Valley galena deposit, one of the largest in the moundbuilding region, was also in this subregion. And canoe traffic on the Missouri River, which flowed through part of this subregion, delivered valuable stones from the Rocky Mountains.

The Fort Ancient site, after which the Fort Ancient cultural subregion is named, is a few miles north of Cincinnati, on a tributary of the Ohio. One group of archaeologists is now investigating the possibility that during the Mississippian Epoch the centers of the Fort Ancient subregion were an important source of forest products for Cahokia. The hypothesis is that not only Fort Ancient, but all the sites that became powerful centers of the various subregions had a special relationship to Cahokia, and that a significant part of that relationship was the delivery of scarce resources to it. Such relationships are easier to trace when the goods involved are imperishable materials such as ores, stones, and shells, but there may well have been similar relationships established by the supply of perishable forest products such as dried meat, deerskins, and furs. If this were the case, the forest products supplied by Fort Ancient may have come from its own subregion as well as from trade with the Iroquois, a people who still live just beyond the Mississippi drainage in western New York.

Although there had been moundbuilding centers in western New York and Ontario during the Hopewellian Period, there are no Mississippian mound sites in these areas, nor is there any evidence of the sort of elite stratification typical of the Mississippian epoch. On the other hand, the ancestors of the Iroquois did adopt many elements of the material culture of the Mississippians and thereby became quite different from their neighbors to the north and east. They lived in nucleated, palisaded villages or towns and were more dependent upon corn than their neighbors to the east. It is clear that they traded with the Fort Ancient subregion, for Ohio cherts and ceramic wares from Fort Ancient and even the Gulf Coast have been found there. And it is possible that the Iroquois, themselves, did not produce all of the forest products they traded. They may have traded whatever desirable goods that they had to the peoples on their periphery in what is now New England in exchange for the latter's forest products, which, combined with their own, were then transported to the Fort Ancient cultural subregion.

The archaeologists investigating these trade relations believe that the concentration of population, especially elite populations, at Cahokia made it impossible for the Middle Mississippian subregion to fill all of this center's needs for forest products, and the ability of the Fort Ancient subregion to supply such goods would explain its prosperity during the Cahokian Era. Marietta, on the Ohio River at the eastern edge of the subregion, may have been the collection point where the Iroquois delivered the goods, which were then stockpiled in the Fort Ancient site. Subsequently they would be transported by canoe down the Ohio and up the Mississippi to Cahokia. The time needed to make such a canoe trip has been calculated to be between thirty and forty-five days. At Cahokia the people from Fort Ancient would have been able to exchange the forest products for goods that came in from other parts of the Mississippian region, both for themselves and for trade to the Iroquois. The trip back to Ohio would have taken longer, for the canoes would have been traveling upstream more of the way.[9]

Participation in the Mississippian realm does not seem to have diminished the prestige or power of the elite lineages who presided over the various subregional centers. Quite the contrary. Evidently their participation in this regionwide phenomenon enabled them to further consolidate their hold over their own locale. There is much evidence to suggest that Mississippian centers drew upon the resources of their hinterlands in unprecedented ways. Many appear to have been surrounded by satellite towns that were in some sense subordinated to them. Among other things, status symbols are concentrated at the main centers and are found in lesser amounts at the satellite sites.

Some investigators have suggested that the Mississippian centers' power over such subordinated satellite communities made it possible for the former to demand tribute in foodstuffs from the latter. They further suggest that this unequal distribution of power led to an unequal division of food and thus a decline in the nutritional levels of people's diets in the subordinated communities. There is some preliminary evidence indicating that in some communities the level of nutrition declined during the Mississippian Period. If this decline occurred in both the centers and in satellite communities, it could be attributed to the transition from harvesting a wide variety of foods from local plants, either cultivated or wild, to depending upon a limited number of domesticated plants, principally corn. So far, however, the evidence suggests that the decline in nutritional levels occurred in some communities, but not in others. Given the small amount of data available on this question so far, the evidence is not conclusive but it does suggest the possibility that people at the centers had access to more or better foods. If true, the unequal division of foods could have been the result of the centers' ceremonial preeminence and their ability to bestow the privilege of participation upon those who came bearing gifts, or of their preeminence within military alliances that were sealed by gift-giving. Or it could have been the result of forced acquisitions from defeated rivals.[10]

Middle Mississippian Outposts in Other Cultural Subregions

One of the more intriguing discoveries that archaeologists have made is that there are sites exhibiting Middle Mississippian cultural features located outside of the Middle Mississippian subregion. These outposts have been identified well inside the boundaries of three other cultural subregions—the Oneota in the north, the Plaquemine in the south, and the Southern Appalachian in the east.[11] They are clearly distinguishable from surrounding sites that belong to the local subregion. Throughout these settlements, one finds only Middle Mississippian characteristics, and there is no evidence of the surrounding local traditions. Although these outposts generally are not large, they do have flat-topped platform mounds where, presumably, their builders performed the central ceremonies. If the people of the local subregion began to build Mississippian-style mounds and carry out Mississippian-style ceremonies only after these Middle Mississippian outposts were established within their subregion, then it could be argued that the outposts were a source of cultural diffusion and contributed to the cultural continuities observable among all the ceremonial centers in the Mississippian Epoch.

It is also possible that these outposts were trading centers established for the purpose of insuring the delivery of local products to the Middle Mississippian subregion. They appear to be located on some of the most important exchange routes, particularly those along which valuable ores and marine shells moved, even including sites on the Gulf coast of Florida. (One is reminded of Begho in West Africa, a settlement of merchants from Mali near the Akan gold fields in present-day Ghana, well outside the reach of Mali's own realm.)

The distribution of Middle Mississippian outposts in the mound-building region does not appear to be random. With regard to the Southeast, their presence could possibly account for the existence of Siouan-speaking communities living amongst much larger groups of peoples speaking Iroquoian, Algonkian, or Muskogean languages. When European settlers and their descendants began to study Native American languages, they were surprised to learn that Siouan-speaking communities could be found from Virginia to Louisiana, at a great distance from the Sioux homelands, which, at least by the eighteenth century, were west of the Mississippi River. One concentration could be found on the Gulf coast near Biloxi in what had been the Plaquemine subregion, and another was located at the headwaters of the Neuse and Santee Rivers, either in or near the Southern Appalachian subregion.[12]

The presence of Siouan-speaking peoples in the Southeast and the knowledge that some of the Dhegihan Sioux valued various kinds of shells and considered them sacred has prompted some people to speculate that the Sioux were originally from eastern coastal areas or the Appalachian Mountains. In support of this idea, these scholars also cite Dhegihan Sioux traditions. These traditions do, in fact, say that the Sioux migrated to their present homelands from the east but not from the Plaquemine or Southern Appalachian subregions. The traditions place the Sioux homeland within the bounds of the Middle Mississippian subregion. Thus a more likely hypothesis would be that it was the Dhegihan Sioux who ruled from Cahokia, the paramount center of the Middle Mississippian subregion, and that they established Siouan outposts in other subregions, including the Plaquemine and Southern Appalachian. This would account for both the presence of the Middle Mississippian outposts and the Siouan-speakers in the Southeast as well as for the specific pattern of their distribution.

Cahokia's Demise

After A.D. 1200 Cahokia and a number of other moundbuilding centers began to decline. The construction of mounds and other structures slowed to a halt, and their populations dwindled. Given the present state of knowledge, it is impossible to say with any certainty why this happened. Some have suggested, based upon general, global trends, that the weather became colder and that this had a negative impact on the viability of these centers. But so far there is little climatic data specific to the Eastern Woodlands, and thus it is not possible to demonstrate such a change. Furthermore, there is some evidence that two other sites in the American Bottom, those now under St. Louis and East St. Louis, were growing at the same time that Cahokia was declining. Although Aztalan (actually a Middle Mississippian outpost) in the Oneota area is an exception, it is clear that many centers flourished even after Cahokia's demise, both in the north and in the south.[13] Nor is there any evidence of warfare or natural disaster that would explain the demise of Cahokia and other sites that declined with it.

It is also been suggested that tuberculosis may have become a problem in some densely populated areas, including Cahokia. (Tuberculosis is an exceedingly old disease, and may have been an exception to the general rule that there were few infectious diseases in the Western Hemisphere.) Archaeologists have found human bones from the Mississippian Period that appear to have been damaged by the disease. And an archaeologist studying Mississippian pottery has suggested that a style of pot that appears in the Middle Mississippian cultural subregion may also give evidence of the presence of tuberculosis. Sometime around 1250, potters in this area began to make "hunch-backed" human effigy pots with a face and torso on one side and a severely rounded upper back with protruding vertebrae on the opposite side (Illustration 36). Such a deformity can be caused by tuberculosis, and it is possible that these pots were made either for ritual healing purposes or for storing herbal remedies specific for the disease.[14]

Another suggestion has been that soils in Cahokia's vicinity may have been depleted and that local forest resources may have become scarce. This would have made Cahokia dependent upon other subregional centers for food and other basic consumption items as well as strategic and ceremonial goods, and such dependency could have threatened its viability. When Cahokia was strong and its resource base secure, other centers may have sought a relationship with it in order to secure their own supply of strategic and ceremonial goods, which would have facilitated the consolidation of their predominance within their own subregion. Such relationships could also have encouraged local

ambitions. And eventually the other subregional centers may have became so secure in their positions that the significance of their relationship to Cahokia declined. Cahokia's dependence upon them for
supplies then would have become a serious vulnerability.

In any case, even after the demise of the Cahokian center and a
decline in regionwide Mississippian ceremonial activity, a number of
successful subregional centers remained. An anthropologist who spe-
cializes on the Southeast has put it well: "We can perhaps use the
analogy of the two-story house in a tornado, where the small, ornate
upper story is blown away, leaving all the lower rooms more or less
intact."[15] It must be emphasized, however, that even though the remaining lower rooms emerged intact, they nevertheless had undergone
significant remodeling during the time that the upper story existed.
What had once been a collection of numerous and relatively small
localities had become consolidated into subregions of considerable
size. Long after Cahokia's demise, Native Americans in the moundbuilding region remained dependent upon the cultivation of corn and
other domesticates from Mesoamerica and South America. They continued to live in palisaded towns and villages. They had participated in
exchange networks almost continental in size, and they were familiar
with paramount power displayed at ceremonial centers. Long after
Cahokia's importance was gone, they maintained elements of the
Mississippian ceremonial, albeit on a smaller scale. Thus when the
Spaniards arrived in the sixteenth century, there were several Great
Suns presiding within the moundbuilding region.

7 CONCLUSION

Prior to 1492, the history of the peoples in the moundbuilding region was unique in many respects. They lived in permanent settlements before they began to cultivate plants. Long before they became dependent upon corn and other crops first domesticated in Mesoamerica, they cultivated indigenous plants, produced their own pottery, and participated in an exchange system of nearly continental proportions. Canoe traffic plied the rivers, and both people and the goods they could carry moved through the woodlands along overland trails. Ceremonial centers knit the various peoples together in a web of grand dimensions. Throughout the region people buried their illustrious dead with the finest goods available from the Rocky Mountains to the beaches of Florida. Later, after A.D. 400, the bow and arrow became the principal weapon, corn became the mainstay of the diet, and palisaded towns became the centers of ceremony and exchange. Thus were the cultural continuities of the moundbuilding region created, without the aid of bronze, iron, chariots, cavalries, or any beast of burden.

The uniqueness of the peoples in the moundbuilding region was related in large part to the abundance of resources in the Eastern Woodlands and to the intricate network of waterways provided by the Mississippi River and its tributaries. The quantity and variety of both plant and animal foods in the river valleys and nearby forests enabled the moundbuilders to become relatively sedentary long before agriculture became important, and it made it possible for them to be highly selective when incorporating new developments. Clearly, by 200 B.C., they knew how to cultivate corn. But they chose to grow it only in small amounts, and for another one thousand years they continued to rely upon gathering or cultivating indigenous plants for food. Although they had only one domesticated animal, the dog, they chose not to domesticate any other animal, not even those that provided their main sources of meat. Even after they became dependent upon cultivated plants, they chose to hunt and to manipulate the supply of these animals in the forest.

After A.D. 900, some peoples lived in towns and in what might appear to be cities: densely populated centers that were supplied by nearby agricultural hamlets and forest hinterlands. The largest of these settlements were home to thousands of people, perhaps even tens of thousands, and all had clearly defined central districts that were often surrounded by a high palisade, where mounds and plazas and the ceremonies performed on them displayed the legitimacy of the peoples' rulers. The settlements also had neighborhoods where artisans lived and worked, where raw materials came in and finely crafted items went out.

When the Spaniards saw some of these centers in the 1500s, they were impressed by them, by the powers of the Great Suns who ruled them, and especially by the number and the skill of the warriors that the Great Suns could mobilize. They admired the handicraft work of the artisans and were amazed by the abundance of food stored in these settlements. Moreover, the centers that the Spaniards saw were by no means the largest that had ever existed in the region. The Spaniards not only came too late to see Cahokia at the peak of its powers, they never even got far enough inland to see the American Bottom.

One suspects that if these centers had been located in any other part of the world, there would be no objection to calling them cities. Yet many U.S. archaeologists still insist that even the most populous cannot be deemed urban because they were the centers of "complex chiefdoms." These archaeologists maintain that chiefdoms, even "complex chiefdoms," never contain cities, and thus, by definition, terms such as "city" and "urban" are inappropriate within this context. It would seem, nevertheless, that it is incumbent upon these archaeologists to explain why the largest centers were not an exception to this rule. Except for the fact that their inhabitants did not possess a written language, the largest centers would seem to fulfill all the usual requirements for urbanity.[1] Alliance networks, not unlike those of the Mississippian Period, can be found in other places, particularly in Africa and Southeast Asia, and there the ceremonial centers, if they fulfill the usual requirements, are referred to as urban. Thus it seems rather strange that ceremonial centers in other parts of the world can qualify as urban while those in Eastern North America cannot.

The Impact of Epidemics

One reason that it is now so difficult to visualize the moundbuilding region as it was before the Columbian voyages—with densely populated towns and villages and with large centers and powerful rulers—is that the region and its peoples have undergone profound and sometimes devastating changes in the last five hundred years. Among these changes, the most important were demographic, for the Native American populations were decimated by the introduction of infectious diseases from the Eastern Hemisphere.[2]

Before 1492, the peoples of the Western Hemisphere lived in an environment that was relatively free of infectious diseases. Peoples in the Eastern Hemisphere, however, had had an entirely different experience. For several thousand years, they had been ravaged by epidemics caused by infectious diseases. When one of these diseases hit a virgin population—a group that had not been exposed to it as children—the disease might carry away as many as one-third of the population. But if an infectious disease follows a common pattern and lingers among the survivors, all the children are exposed to it, and those that survive grow into adults immune to the disease. By 1492, commercial networks had so knit the Eastern Hemisphere together that, with almost no exceptions, people from one end to the other had shared all their diseases insofar as various ecological settings made that possible. They therefore shared a common set of infectious diseases and, even more importantly, they shared a common set of immunities.[3]

Consequently, what the European ships delivered to the Americas were not just those diseases born in Europe, but a hemispherewide collection that had been more than three thousand years in the making. No person in North or South America was immune to any of them. The peoples of the Western Hemisphere were exposed to these diseases one after the other in rapid succession, and the result was devastation, a veritable holocaust that in densely populated areas sometimes killed as many as 90 percent of the people. In the millennia prior to 1492, the peoples of the Eastern Hemisphere had paid a high price for their invulnerability to so many diseases, but after 1492 that invulnerability would allow one small group of them, those from the hemisphere's North Atlantic shores, to possess most of the Western Hemisphere.

The impact of epidemic disease on the Mexican and Andean empires is well known, but few are aware of what happened in the Mississippian region. Epidemics had begun to take their toll even before 1539, when de Soto's expedition began its exploration of "Florida." For example, when the Spaniards reached Cofitachequi (in what is now South Carolina) in 1540, they found that it had been hit by an epidemic about two years before their arrival. This center, which had once been populous, was empty and overgrown with weeds. While going through the ruins, some of de Soto's men found a number of Spanish manufactures, and they asked a neighboring people how these items had reached Cofitachequi. The reply was that the goods had come from Christians who many years before had resided at a port two days' journey away. The Spaniards then realized that the goods had come from an ill-fated colony established on the South Carolina coast by Lucas Vázquez de Ayllón in 1526. Ayllón himself had died upon arrival, and eventually all those who had come with him either died or departed the region. Nevertheless, it appears that this group of would-be colonists had remained long enough to establish their germs in South Carolina.[4]

But Cofitachequi was still an exception in the mid-sixteenth century. As the de Soto expedition moved further inland and traversed the woodlands from what is now the Carolinas to the eastern part of Texas (see Map 12), it found many densely populated valleys. De Soto's expedition did not go far enough north to see the American Bottom, but it did see many flourishing centers and towns in the Central Mississippi Valley, a rich bottomland between the mouths of the Ohio and the Arkansas rivers. In fact, no European ever saw the Cahokia site or the American Bottom until 1673, when two Frenchmen, Jacques Marquette and Louis Joliet, departed from present-day Canada in search of a passage to India. Native Americans had told them that the Great River eventually flowed into a large body of water. Hoping that this was the Pacific Ocean, the French explorers canoed down the Mississippi from the north.

It is clear from Marquette's account of their voyage that catastrophic changes had taken place in the American Bottom and the Central Mississippi Valley in the 131 years since de Soto's expedition had traversed the moundbuilding region. Between the mouths of the

88

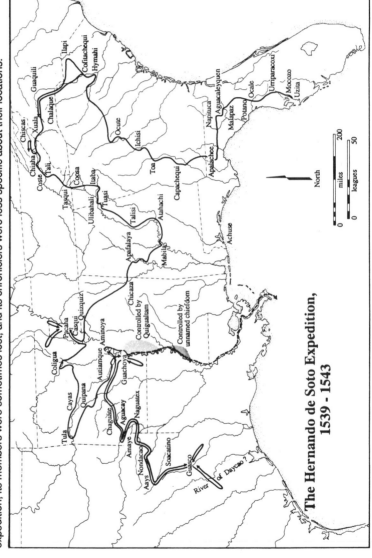

Map 12. **Route of the de Soto Expedition.** In recent years, much progress has been made in determining de Soto's route. This map, made by anthropologist Charles Hudson and his associates in 1991, reflects recent scholarship on the subject. The routes that the expedition took when in present-day Texas are still not well understood. On this part of the expedition, its members were sometimes lost, and its chroniclers were less specific about their locations.

The Hernando de Soto Expedition, 1539 - 1543

Illinois and the Arkansas rivers they saw not a single person originally from these bottomlands. The only people that they came across were two small settlements of Tuscaroras, whose home at that time was in central North Carolina. (The Tuscaroras are an Algonquian-speaking people, linguistically related to the Cherokee and the Iroquois. In 1711, several decades after Marquette and Joliet canoed down the Mississippi, they were dealt a severe military defeat by a coalition of Cherokees and English colonists in South Carolina. Thereafter, most Tuscaroras left North Carolina, sought refuge in the north with the Iroquois, and joined their Confederacy.)

One of the Tuscarora settlements was located a short way upriver from the American Bottom; the other was located just south of it in the Central Mississippi Valley. Thus in 1673 the entire American Bottom, once the most populous place in Eastern North America, was completely devoid of human life, and the rivers' shores had been overgrown by wild cane and cypress trees. The Central Mississippi Valley also would have been completely empty had it not been for the one Tuscarora village within it. It was not until the Frenchmen approached the mouth of the Arkansas River that they saw a large village. It belonged to the Quapaw, a people who speak a Dhegihan Sioux language.[5]

Once they had reached the Quapaw, Marquette and Joliet began to observe villages and towns with abundant stores of corn, similar to those that the Spaniards had seen so many years before. They were duly impressed by the local agriculture and even reported that the Quapaw were able to harvest three crops a year. And though Marquette and Joliet had great difficulty communicating with people who spoke a Dhegihan Sioux language, they did find out that the Mississippi River flowed into the Gulf of Mexico and not into the Pacific. Once they knew that the Great River would not take them to the Pacific but would deliver them into the hands of the Spanish, then the dominant power at the Mississippi delta, they turned around and went back to Canada the same way that they had come.

The archaeological record confirms what Marquette and Joliet observed: that after 1550, much of the Middle Mississippian subregion was devoid of people. The most likely explanation for this phenomenon is that its population had been decimated by disease, and that the survivors had abandoned its bottomlands. These densely populated areas, once the heart of the moundbuilding region, would have been exceedingly vulnerable to infectious diseases since, as a rule, epidemics are most lethal among densely settled virgin populations.

It is quite possible that the de Soto expedition left a trail of infectious diseases behind it, and any one of these diseases could easily have spread north into the American Bottom. Its settlements were at the hub of an extensive exchange network, and people were constantly coming and going. Thus there was no need for Europeans to carry the germs into the American Bottom. Germs planted anywhere within the moundbuilding region would have been quite capable of finding a local human host to transport them to this hub along indigenous exchange routes.

Another possible explanation for the abandonment of the Middle Mississippian bottomlands is that they became infested with malaria as early as the sixteenth century. Prior to 1492, there was no malaria in the Western Hemisphere, but not long after the Columbian voyages some American mosquitoes did become hosts to the parasite that causes this disease. The ponds, lakes, and low-lying marshes of the silt-laden bottoms, where the land is so fertile and so easily cultivated, provide an ideal habitat for mosquitoes. Once the mosquitoes became infested with malaria, they made such places uninhabitable. There is no doubt that by 1800 a deadly form of malaria was present in many parts of the American Bottom and that for this reason much of it was left empty, even by European-American settlers, until the middle of the nineteenth century.[6] The only question is whether or not it became malarial as early as 1550. If so, the presence of this disease is the most likely cause for the transformation of densely populated bottomlands with field after field of carefully tended corn into the uninhabited thickets of cane and cypress that Marquette and Joliet observed.

Since there is no certainty regarding whose ancestors once lived at Cahokia, it is difficult to say precisely what happened to those who abandoned the Middle Mississippian valleys. Nevertheless, circumstantial evidence points to Siouan-speaking peoples. At some point, both the Siouan tribes of the north and the Dhegihan Sioux tribes to their south began to move westward. By the eighteenth century, they had become a part of a new Plains culture established with the aid of the mustang (wild horse). Although they still did some farming, the hunting of wild buffalo herds had become central to their way of life.

Marquette and Joliet did find one Dhegihan Sioux people, the

Quapaw, still living on the Mississippi in 1673, apparently unscathed by whatever force had emptied the bottomlands to their north. But their good fortune came to an abrupt end some twenty-five years later. In 1698, they were visited by Thomas Welch, a British fur trader from South Carolina. His business was prospering, and in an effort to expand his supplies, he journeyed westward all the way to the Mississippi River, far outside the English sphere of influence. No sooner had he reached the Quapaw towns than a smallpox epidemic broke out. In one town, half the men, most of the women, and all the children died. Those who were still alive were too weak to care for the dying or hunt for meat.[7]

In 1713, further south on the eastern bank of the Mississippi River (in what is now northwestern Mississippi), a group of Frenchmen finally did encounter a Mississippian people, the Natchez. (Many authorities now believe the Natchez were the descendants of the people of Quigaltam, whose Great Sun attacked de Soto's expedition in 1542.) Some two hundred years after the Spaniards first set foot in the moundbuilding region, the Natchez still maintained many of the traditional ceremonies, and a Great Sun still presided over their center. The French obtained permission to establish a trading post on Natchez territory, and French descriptions of their hosts have provided archaeologists, historians, and anthropologists with invaluable material about the culture of at least one moundbuilding center. Unfortunately, good relations between the two peoples did not last, and war broke out in 1724. In 1731, the French (with the aid of Choctaw allies and European cannons) defeated the Natchez. Casualties in the war were high, and in its aftermath the French executed many survivors and sold about four hundred people into slavery in the Caribbean. Those who escaped from the French eventually took refuge among other southeastern tribes.[8]

English-speaking colonists saw even less of the traditional Mississippian cultures than did the French. When the British came to the Atlantic shores of what they would call Virginia and New England, they were arriving at places that had not been part of the moundbuilding region, often at places already devastated by epidemics. It was not until they had established coastal enclaves in the Carolinas and Georgia that they came close to any moundbuilding centers. Even as late as King George III's Proclamation of 1763, the British government still could hope to keep its own colonists east of the Appalachians and away from its Native American allies, who were located in what had once been the moundbuilding region. Thus, with almost no exceptions, English-speaking colonists did not see any Mississippian centers until after the centers' populations had been reduced by disease and mound-building activities had ceased.

Until the nineteenth century, the descendants of the Mississippians and other Native American peoples living on the Plains west of the Mississippi River were less vulnerable to epidemics. They were relatively distant from large concentrations of European-Americans, and due to their acquisition of the horse and their new, more mobile way of life, they could flee from a place at the first report of an epidemic. After 1800, however, their relative security came to an end. As steamboats began churning up the rivers and railroads began stretching across the Plains, the number of European-Americans on the Plains multiplied exponentially. Native American hunting grounds became contested, and the buffalo herds shrank. Warfare and hostilities increased, and so did the number of U.S. soldiers. The likelihood of exposure to disease increased, epidemics came upon them without warning, and there was no safe place to which they might flee.

Just how devastating the Plains epidemics of the nineteenth century could be is indicated by a well-documented outbreak of smallpox in the 1830s. One group hit by this epidemic were the Mandan, Native American fur traders who had had a close relationship with the French during the colonial period and who had remained friendly and hospitable to whites after the U.S. purchase of Louisiana in 1803. The artist George Catlin stayed with them in 1832. His painting of a chunkey game shows a tall, healthy, and vigorous Mandan crowd cheering on the players. But on June 19, 1837, an American Fur Company steamship stopped at a port on the Missouri River near where some two thousand Mandan people lived. Among its passengers were three Native Americans ill with smallpox, and the Mandan became infected with the disease.

The first Mandan smallpox casualty occurred on July 14, and by August 22 between thirty-five and fifty people were dying every day. By September 800 people had died. When the epidemic was over, only some 120 or 130 people were still alive, and many of these were elders who had had smallpox when they were young. Nevertheless, some Mandan survived. Today they are a small group, many of whom live amongst other tribes on the Fort Berthold Reservation in North Dakota.[9]

Atlantic Powers

The peoples of the moundbuilding region were not unique with regard to the devastation visited upon them by epidemics and war. However, they were unusual in that some of them became important international actors within the eighteenth-century Atlantic realm. After the Mississippian bottomlands were abandoned, the peoples who lived on the circumference of the moundbuilding region turned away from the old centers and faced outward, toward the oceanic networks of the European powers. Some were quite successful in developing ways to cope with the catastrophic changes in their world and actually profited from opportunities afforded by the presence of Eastern Hemisphere peoples and the new oceanic trade routes. Among the most notable of these were the peoples who once had lived at the four corners of the moundbuilding region: the Iroquois (whose ancestors had been Hopewellian and who had had close contacts with the Mississippian networks) in the northeast corner, the Cherokee in the southeast, the Lakota and Dakota Sioux in the northwest, and the Osage in the southwest.

In general, this pattern has been little remarked upon, but one demographer, Henry F. Dobyns, has noted that by the eighteenth century the predominant Native Americans powers in the southeast were not coastal peoples but uplanders. He attributes this phenomenon to the fact that peoples on the coast were more vulnerable to epidemic diseases and European firepower, and he notes that those who lived along the rivers, slow-moving as they approached the coast, would have been especially vulnerable to water-related diseases such as typhoid and malaria. Uplanders, on the other hand, who lived some distance from the coast, would be less vulnerable to such threats, although by no means immune. This, he suggests, explains why the peoples of the Gulf Coast basin became relatively weak and the uplanders eventually expanded down onto lands that had once belonged to coastal peoples.[10]

No doubt this observation does help explain why the Iroquois and the Cherokee emerged as powers in the East. The Cherokee heartland was in the southern Appalachians, just far enough away from the Atlantic coast to provide some protection, but close enough to Charleston, South Carolina, to establish a relationship with the British. The Iroquois did not live in the mountains, but their lands were separated from the Atlantic coast by the northern end of the Appalachians. They were thus outside the coastal drainage area, and this would have offered some protection from water-borne diseases. At the same time, the Hudson River, which ran along their eastern frontier, provided access to colonial ports on the coast. Likewise, the relative safety of the Plains peoples from epidemics, attributable to their ability to disperse in times of danger, would help to explain the power of the Sioux and the Osage.

However, there may be yet another important reason for this pattern. These eighteenth-century Native American powers were all descendants of peoples who had been a part of the moundbuilding region. They, in particular, responded to the presence of the Europeans and the extraordinary European ocean-crossing exchange networks. And they did this in much the same way that their ancestors had once responded to the Great Suns. They understood paramount power and the advantages of allying with it. They understood the significance of having access to unusual strategic and ceremonial goods. And they had been part of a tradition that emphasized diplomatic and ceremonial activities. It is not surprising that they were the ones who established mutually beneficial relationships with the Europeans and used these connections to enhance their positions locally. Thus it would appear that until the nineteenth century, when the industrial revolution drastically altered the global balance of power, their pre-1492 heritage served them well.

Backdoors in World History

The Spaniards first approached the moundbuilding region through Florida, long its front door, and they were defeated. By the end of the sixteenth century, they had to content themselves with the Florida peninsula and a narrow sphere of influence along the Gulf coast, places that sea power alone could secure. Later, however, they would approach overland from the southwest, as would the French from the north, and the English from the east. Thus these ocean-coming powers posed unprecedented challenges and opportunities, not directly to the Mississippian heartland, but to peoples on the moundbuilding region's periphery who had previously been unexposed to such temptations.

Before 1492, in the absence of any long-distance Atlantic seaways, the great centers of the region had been on its rivers, and its peoples had faced inward toward the great riverine centers. The divided and contending Europeans, however, came through the backdoors and thereby provoked a radical transformation of the Mississippian patterns. The peoples of its rim did an about-face toward the new oceanic powers. Even if the old Mississippian bottomlands had not been infested with disease, their regional networks would have been pulled apart.

Eastern North America was not the only place in the world that ocean-borne Europeans arrived at the back door. Nor was it the only place where old networks were turned inside out to face the oceans and the paramount powers that sailed them. Wherever European voyagers were the first to develop an ocean route, there were similar transformations. West Africa's grandest empires, for example, had always been oriented northward toward the Saharan Desert, a great ocean of sand across which all significant international traffic had come. The political and military structures of Ghana, Mali, and Songhai had been shaped by trade routes designed to meet the "port" cities on the desert's southern edge. Thus the creation by Portugal in the fifteenth century of an Atlantic route between Lisbon and the southern coast of West Africa caused a dramatic change in trading patterns. Valuable commodities, especially gold, that had always gone north were drawn thereafter to the south. The great empires on the savannahs became a thing of the past, and for the first time in West African history kingdoms proliferated in the south and contended for power over the best roads to the region's southern coast.

The reason that the new Atlantic routes to West Africa and Eastern North America had such a profound and far-reaching impact upon the internal balance of power within these regions was that the routes were altogether new, not merely new to European ships. For various geographical and climatic reasons, they had remained unused for long distance travel by anyone until the European voyages of the fifteenth century. Although both regions had long been linked to other regions within their own hemispheres, the routes that linked them to other places did not go over the oceans, and harbors on their oceanic coasts had never served as gates into the regions. Thus prior to the European voyages, the Atlantic coasts of West Africa and Eastern North America had never had direct access to important long-distance exchange networks, and they had never been major seats of power within their regions. The political and exchange patterns of both regions had formed around features other than the oceans. Their most powerful centers, those places where their peoples and their strengths were concentrated, were not on the coasts but far in the interior.

The Europeans who came across the oceans approached these regions through what had been the backdoors and thereby challenged the traditional centers of power in totally unprecedented ways and places. Suddenly, the centers' resources and defenses were concentrated in the wrong places. On the other hand, the new ocean routes opened up unprecedented opportunities, as well as new dangers, for those peoples who were located on what had once been the regions' peripheries. Now they could contend for control over the roads that led to the oceanic ports that would become the regions' front doors.

Because all the new Atlantic powers came to the backdoors (except for the Spaniards who came to Eastern North America before 1550), their initial impressions of these regions were usually mistaken. The Europeans were unaware that the places they saw first were the far side of a periphery and were not typical of the region as a whole. Furthermore, the Europeans rarely came to realize their mistake, for by the time that many of them did become acquainted with the interior areas, the power and the prestige of the old centers had already been undermined.

The profound changes brought about in Eastern North America and West Africa by the new oceanic roads that the Europeans created can be contrasted with the much less significant impact that the arrival of European ships had on regional patterns of organization in places that fronted the Indian Ocean and in Southeast and East Asia. In 1497, after the Portuguese ships had rounded the southern end of Africa and sailed into the ports of East Africa, they were no longer opening up a new maritime road. Rather, they were embarking upon oceanic routes that had linked East Africa to southern China and Japan, and all ports in between, for more than a thousand years. The presence of European ships did not present such a fundamental challenge to the political and economic structures of these regions. They had long since adapted to such routes. While it is true that the Portuguese did do serious damage to commercial traffic on these oceans and seas, local traders eventually found ways to circumvent Portuguese seapower. Thus in most areas, European powers did not have much of an impact on the hinterlands of these ports until the eighteenth or nineteenth centuries.

The Conquest of the Moundbuilding Region

Native Americans who were the descendants of the Mississippians continued to possess the moundbuilding region until the nineteenth century. Only then were they conquered. It is true that the region had been utterly transformed soon after the Europeans arrived in the Western Hemisphere, that various European powers had claimed exclusive rights over various parts of it, and that a few small coastal enclaves were actually controlled by Europeans. Nevertheless, it is possible to say that at the turn of the nineteenth century almost the entire region was still under Native American control. But between 1820 and 1870, in just fifty years, Native Americans lost all their lands from the Appalachians to the Rocky Mountains.

A considerable amount of energy has gone into elucidating the causes of their defeat. The reasons given often seem to imply that if the Native Americans had been different or had done something differently, they might have made a more successful response to the challenges they faced and they might not have suffered so terribly. But such perspectives on the events of the nineteenth century underestimate the impact of the industrial revolution and the totally unprecedented power and prestige that it conferred on the Atlantic powers and the new United States. The Mississippians and other Native Americans were not the only ones to fall before the tools of empire wrought by the industrial revolution.[11] They went down in the best of company. At more or less the same time, in the Eastern Hemisphere from the Atlantic to the Pacific, powers that had been among the grandest in the world were signing the "unequal treaties" just as the Native Americans were. They, too, had their sovereignty compromised and their territory taken.

People all around the globe were contending with constantly improving firearms technologies, steamboats, railroads, and new and amazingly fast communications technologies. In the nineteenth century, it did not make much difference what strategies the nonindustrial nations pursued. Those who went down included both those who clung to their traditions and those who emulated the West.

China, for example, was one of the largest and best integrated states in the world, but neither the prestige nor the power of the Chinese empire could save it from defeat by a Britain newly armed by the industrial revolution with iron gunboats and muskets equipped with percussion caps. The Chinese and many other peoples who were defeated repeatedly in the late eighteenth and the nineteenth centuries had been literate much longer than the northwestern Europeans. In fact, they had been the inventors of many of the devices that helped to create Western European hegemony. The Indians, the Native American's namesakes in Asia, had invented the very numbers and the mathematics that underlay the beginnings of modern science and technology. They had been the first to domesticate cotton and to develop the technology for printing and dyeing cotton textiles. They were the first to crystallize sugar and turn it into a lucrative international commodity. The lateen sail (without which the Portuguese could not have explored the West African coast) and critical astronomical data had come from the Arabs, and the compass, gunpowder, and printing had come from China. Such facts made little difference, except that after these Eastern Hemisphere nations were defeated, they got called backward instead of primitive.

Although many peoples around the globe were being overwhelmed by the new technologies, it was the Native Americans in what is now the continental United States who alone had to absorb about 70 percent of the phenomenal population explosion that occurred among Europeans and their descendants in the nineteenth century. Between 1800 and 1900, the European population grew at a rate of 106 percent, almost twice the rate in the rest of the world (63 percent). During these same years, Europe exported some 50 million permanent emigrants, of whom some 35 million went to the United States. And they, too, reproduced rapidly in their new homes. In this period, the world population of European origin increased by about 166 percent, from 210 million at the beginning to 560 million at the end. While the Native American population was still declining, the U.S. population grew from 5.3 million in 1800 to 76 million in 1900.[12]

No one else in the world had to contend with such a powerful demographic force. Great waves of people flooded what had once been the moundbuilding region and thereby undermined the Native Americans' economic base. In the 1830s, when the English demand for cotton sent its price soaring and the U.S. government could no longer contain settlers' desire for the cotton fields of Native American peoples in the Southeast, the U.S. Army deported from their lands approximately 100,000 people, all of them descendants of Mississippians.[13] They were deposited west of the Mississippi River, on lands that were once the territory of other Mississippian peoples and which sometimes the latter's descendants still claimed.

Nor was it simply a matter of hordes of European-American settlers coveting land. A relatively new and fragile U.S. government was frightened by the knowledge that the Native American powers on its borders were independent actors within the international arena quite capable of allying with its enemies. In the War of 1812, General (later President) Andrew Jackson had enlisted Cherokee aid to defeat the Creeks so that he could get to New Orleans and attack the British. Although Jackson gladly received the aid of the Cherokees, he also knew that their principal loyalties were to their own nation and not the United States. In his mind, the deportations, including the Cherokee's Trail of Tears, were a matter not only of land; they were also a matter of national security.[14]

By 1870, the Native American peoples on the Plains, including those that had once been moundbuilders, had also been defeated, and the new boundaries of the United States were secure. The reservations where Native Americans had been concentrated were essentially colonial possessions located within the new U.S. boundaries, and the U.S. government's policies toward the Native Americans were quite similar to those of the European powers and Japan toward their colonies. In fact, U.S. policies most resembled those pursued by Japan in Korea, as the Japanese attempted to undermine the Koreans' sense of identity and to convince them that their nation was rightfully a part of Japan. Missionaries were sent to the Native American reservations, just as they were sent overseas, and they joined the U.S. government in a concerted effort to uplift the Native Americans by attacking their languages and their religions. The U.S. Congress also passed the Dawes Act (1887). This law was ostensibly an effort to "civilize" the Native Americans by forcing them to divide up their land, which was still owned communally by the tribes, and turn it into privately owned farms. But, as predicted by its critics, the law served mainly to relieve the Native Americans of much of their remaining land. From the aftermath of World War I through the years of World War II, the U.S. government carried out "reforms" quite similar to those carried out by the Europeans and Japan in their colonies.

But unlike their counterparts in the rest of the colonial world, Native Americans in the United States did not regain full sovereignty over their lands in the period of decolonization that followed World War II. Their demographic defeat was irreversible. Nevertheless, the descendants of the moundbuilders are still a part of American society, and our vision of the past will be faulty until we know their history, before and after 1492. In a variety of ways, it was their culture, their roots, and their power that shaped Eastern North American history for the first three centuries of the post-Columbian era. And after their defeat in the nineteenth century, they, along with other Native Americans, have begun to recover their place in our society and have become a unique part of the twentieth century's Third World voice. They are now and always have been a significant part of the American story. It is a shame that most of us do not know it.

FOR FURTHER READING

Ancient Art of the American Woodland Indians, by David Brose, James A. Brown, and David W. Penny (New York: Abrams, 1985) provides an excellent chronological survey of arts and crafts in the moundbuilding region. The pieces are beautifully photographed and carefully documented, and the narrative provides a scholarly summary of their social context and symbolic meaning. Those interested in the Southeast, before and after contact, should see Charles Hudson's *Southeastern Indians* (Knoxville: University of Tennessee, 1976). The best general account of Cahokia is Melvin Fowler's *Cahokia, Ancient Capital of the Midwest* (Reading, MA: Addison-Wesley Publishing Co., 1974). Those interested in the Lower Mississippi Valley and Louisiana should write to the Division of Archaeology, P.O. Box 44247, Baton Rouge, LA 70804, for a list of publications, which include the essay by Robert W. Neuman and Nancy W. Hawkins on Louisiana prehistory and the essay by Jon L. Gibson on Poverty Point. Those interested in Illinois sites can write to the Center for Archaeological Investigations, Southern Illinois University, Carbondale, IL 62901, for a list of the center's publications. Recent archaeological textbooks are Brian M. Fagan, *Ancient North America: The Archaeology of a Continent* (London and New York: Thames and Hudson, 1991), and Jesse D. Jennings, *Prehistory of North America*, 3rd Edition (Mountain View, CA: Mayfield Publishing Co., 1989).

NOTES

1. Introduction

1. Nineteenth-century descriptions and estimates of the number of mounds can be found in Squire and Davis (1973 reprint) and Cyrus Thomas (1985 reprint).
2. Neuman and Hawkins, 1987: 6.
3. Fowler, 1969a: 7.
4. Silverberg, 1986: 33, 43; Tesser and Hudson, 1991: 43.
5. Dobyns, 1983: 42; Thornton, 1987: 32; Ramenovsky, 1987; all of the above are discussed in Fagan, 1991: 432.
6. Bakeless, 1961: 283, 320.
7. Bakeless, 1961: 327–28, 339.
8. Dobyns, 1983: 258; Covey, 1961: 11.
9. Hudson, 1976: 102–19.
10. Lewis, 1907: 203–4.

2. The Archaic Context

1. Fagan, 1991: 74.
2. Fagan, 1991: 95, 110, 307, 316; Smith, 1986: 5, 15; Gibson, 1985: 16; Griffin, 1967: 178; Streuver and Holton, 1979: 165, 209.
3. Griffin, 1967: 180.
4. Hudson, 1976: 157–59.
5. Information concerning the preference for deer ribs and the construction of houses comes from Streuver and Holton, 1979: 141–43, 211. All other material comes from Fagan, 1991: 320, 324 and Smith, 1987: 26–27.
6. Information regarding copper comes from Griffin, 1967: 180 and Penny, 1985: 29. Other information comes from Smith, 1986: 30–31.
7. Walthall, 1981: 6, 36; Walthall, 1979: 247.
8. The material regarding Florida, including pottery, comes from Milanich and Fairbank, 1980: 61, 146–52, and Dobyns, 1983: 129–30. Other information

regarding pottery can be found in Fagan, 1991: 355 and Meggers, 1972: 38–39, 47. Creek hunters are described by Hudson, 1976: 129. Other material comes from Griffin, 1967: 180; Smith, 1986: 30–31; Smith, 1987: 8, 14, 28, 37; Streuver and Holton, 1979: 52; and Fagan, 1991: 347, 355.

9. Information regarding the Koster site comes from Streuver and Holton, 1979: 213. For the uses of gourds see Hudson, 1976: 294 and Dobyns, 1983: 129–30. The list of domesticates was compiled from Asch and Asch, 1985: 153–95; Hudson, 1976: 182–3, 294; and Streuver and Holton, 1979: 123–26, 232. Other information is from Smith, 1986: 30–31 and Smith, 1987: 8; 14, 28, 37.

10. McNeill, 1976: 178.

3. Poverty Point

1. Gibson, 1985: 1–4, 9.
2. Neuman and Hawkins, 1987: 6.
3. Gibson, 1985: 3, 10.
4. Neuman and Hawkins, 1987: 10.
5. Gibson, 1985: 9–11; Neuman and Hawkins, 1987: 11.
6. Ford and Webb, 1956; Gibson, 1973; and Penny, 1985:27–28. Some have questioned the population figures estimated for this site on the basis that they are high for the time period. However, since the site itself is atypical of the period, it would seem reasonable to accept the estimates of the archaeologists who have worked there.
7. Gibson, 1985: 4–7, 12–14.
8. Smith, 1986: 35.
9. Streuver and Holton, 1979: 228.
10. Gibson, 1985: 16–23; Smith, 1986: 33.
11. Asch and Asch, 1985: 195.
12. Gibson, 1985: 4, 24–26, 31; and Neuman and Hawkins, 1987: 12.
13. Walthall, 1981: 37.
14. Gibson, 1985: 3, 22, 30–32.
15. Milanich and Fairbanks, 1980: 62–3.

4. Adena-Hopewell

1. Fagan, 1991: 370; Griffin, 1967: 183.
2. Squier and Davis, (1973 reprint): 3–4.
3. Bakeless, 1961: 283–86.
4. Griffin, 1967: 180; Streuver and Holton, 1979: 228. Information regarding the Central Mississippi Valley comes from Morse and Morse, 1982: 137.
5. Squier and Davis, (1973 reprint): 4.
6. Fagan, 1991: 361; Griffin, 1967: 183; Brose, 1985: 53. The description of the serpent mound is from Morgan, 1980: 23.
7. Prufer, 1964: 90, 98; Brose, 1985: 67; Walthall, 1979: 205.
8. Griffin, 1967: 180; Walthall, 1979: 247; Prufer, 1964: 90.
9. Griffin, 1967: 182–83; Smith, 1987: 38; Hudson, 1976: 292; Prufer, 1964: 90.

Although some have expressed doubt about the early dates for corn in Florida and southern Georgia, it would seem that the benefit of the doubt should go to those who have worked at the sites and obtained the radiocarbon dates. The coastal areas in and around Florida seem to be atypical in many respects, and thus these dates seem reasonable within the local context, even if they are atypical for the entire region.

10. Brose, 1985: 51; Streuver and Holton, 1979: 188–90; Lallo, Rose, and Armelagos, 1980: 205–6. Information about the transformation in seeds comes from Smith, 1987: 14.

11. Walthall, 1979: 200, 205–7, 247–50; Walthall, 1981: 44. The information regarding high-altitude trails comes from Hudson, 1976: 314.

12. Hudson, 1976: 56; Johnson, 1979: 92.

13. Walthall, 1979: 205; Hudson, 1976: 62, 80–81.

14. Goad, 1978: 212–15.

15. Hall, 1980: 436; Fagan, 1991: 383; Prufer, 1964: 90; Goad, 1978: 206.

5. Cahokia and Other Mississippian Centers

1. Fowler, 1969a: 1; Fowler, 1975b: 91, 94; Fowler, 1974: 6.

2. Eggan, 1952: 44–45.

3. The date for platform mounds in Georgia is from Hudson, 1976: 73. The date for Florida is from Milanich and Fairbanks, 1980: 187. The date for platform mounds in the Mississippi Valley is from Morgan, 1980: 120. Some archaeologists would not classify the earliest platform mounds in Georgia and Florida as Mississippian. Because their definition is based on characteristics of sites in the Mississippi Valley, it tends to exclude sites older than A.D. 700. Because the dates are early, some also raise doubts about the radiocarbon dates assigned to the earliest platform mounds in Georgia and Florida. However, since the radiocarbon dates so far obtained for pottery and corn also indicate that they appear in these southern locales earlier than elsewhere, it would seem that the earlier date for platform mounds fits the local pattern. Since so many of the dates from southern locales are unusually early, it would seem, once again, that the benefit of the doubt should go to those who have worked at the sites. One has to consider the possibility that new radiocarbon tests, should they be made, might actually confirm these early dates.

4. Hudson, 1976: 110–11; Fowler, 1975b: 96–100; Fowler, 1978: 461–67.

5. For information regarding the sites in Florida see Milanich and Fairbanks, 1980: 183–7. Regarding Oklahoma see Hamilton, Hamilton, and Chapman, 1974: 176. Other information is from Hudson, 1976: 126.

6. Lathrap, 1985: 354. The origin of this corn, an eight-rowed variety, is controversial, but I find Lathrop's arguments convincing.

7. Hudson, 1976: 80–81, 292–93.

8. Brown, 1981: 3–5.

9. Information about galena comes from Walthall, 1981: 44. The information about chert sources and the description of the chunkey game are from Fowler, 1975: 98. Spanish descriptions of local technologies are from Lewis, 1907: 208, 225, 251.

10. Lewis, 1907: 208, 209, 216, 226, 231, 247.

11. Morgan, 1980: 49, 114–17.

12. Fowler, 1974: 3; Smith, 1978: 460.
13. Lewis, 1907: 213, 216.
14. Fowler, 1975b: 91, 94; Fowler, 1978: 457; Hudson, 1976: 92–93.
15. Information about Mississippian elite burials comes from Fowler, 1974: 22. Information on the Natchez comes from Hudson, 1976: 206–9. The material on Florida is in Dobyns, 1983: 53. For information from the Spanish accounts see Lewis, 1907: 216 and Varner and Varner, 1988: 279, 334.
16. Emerson, 1982: 5, 10.
17. Hudson, 1976: 73, 209, 255.
18. Lewis, 1907: 234.
19. Hudson, 1976: 329.
20. Lewis, 1907: 212.
21. Lewis, 1907: 203–4, 210–13.
22. The description of Quigaltam is from Varner and Varner, 1988: 495–96, 539, 552. All other material regarding the confrontation between de Soto and Quigaltam is from Lewis, 1907: 216–29. The quotations are from Lewis, 1907: 228–29.
23. Lewis, 1907: 203–4.
24. Hodge, 1907: 85–86.
25. Lewis, 1907: 210, 251.
26. Lewis, 1907: 256–57.

6. Subregions, Outposts, and the Decline of Cahokia

1. Griffin, 1967: 185.
2. Morgan, 1980: 114; Hudson, 1976: 85, 93.
3. Information on the location of shells and ores is from Goad, 1978: 179, 215. Other material is from Brown, 1985: 115.
4. Dobyns, 1983: 81–88, 112–16, 127–30, 259.
5. Lewis, 1907: 223–24, 247.
6. Nassaney, 1989: 2–3.
7. *Caddoan Mounds*, 1984: 5–10.
8. Griffin, 1967: 185.
9. Dincauze and Hasenstab, 1989: 1, 5, 8.
10. Material regarding the consolidation of subregions is from Morse and Morse, 1982: 314. Information about the decline in nutrition is from Goodman and Armelagos, 1985: 18.
11. Griffin, 1967: 185.
12. Mooney, 1894: 9–10, Pl. I.
13. Dincauze and Hasenstab, 1989: 5, 8.
14. Lee, 1992.
15. Hudson, 1976: 206.

7. Conclusion

1. O'Brien, 1972: 189–97.
2. Morse and Morse, 1982: 314.

3. McNeill, 1976: 176.

4. Tesser and Hudson, 1991: 46; Lewis, 1907: 174; Morse and Morse, 1982: 314.

5. Morse and Morse, 1982: 284; Bakeless, 1961: 330, 340.

6. Bakeless, 1961: 336.

7. Bakeless, 1961: 341; Morse and Morse, 1982: 284, 317–18.

8. Hudson, 1976: 440; Nash, 1982: 110.

9. Dobyns, 1983: 95–99, 309; Hudson, 1976: 425; Morse and Morse, 1982: 314.

10. Dobyns, 1983: 307.

11. Headrick, 1981: 11–12. This volume provides an excellent discussion of nineteenth-century advances in medicine and technology and the manner in which they became tools of empire in Asia and Africa. Unfortunately, Headrick does not include any examples from North America.

12. Vidal-Naquet, 1987: 214–15.

13. Mahon, 1988: 159–60.

14. Green, 1982: 43–47.

BIBLIOGRAPHY

Anderson, James. (1969) "A Cahokia Palisade Sequence," in Fowler, 1969b: 89–99.

Asch, David L., and Nancy E. Asch (1985) "Prehistoric Plant Cultivation in West-Central Illinois," in Ford, 1985: 149–204.

Bakeless, John. (1961) *The Eyes of Discovery: America as Seen by the First Explorers.* New York: Dover Publications, Inc..

Bareis, Charles J., and James W. Porter (Eds.). (1984) *American Bottom Archaeology.* Urbana, IL: University of Illinois Press.

Borah, W. (1976) "The Historical Demography of Aboriginal and Colonial North America: An Attempt at Perspective," in Denevan, 1976: 13–34.

Brose, David. (1979) "A Speculative Model of the Role of Exchange in the Prehistory of the Eastern Woodlands," in Brose and Greber, 1979: 3–8.

———. (1985) "The Woodland Period," in Brose, Brown, and Penney, 1985: 43–92.

Brose, David, James A. Brown, and David W. Penney. (1985) *Ancient Art of the American Woodland Indians.* New York: Harry N. Abrams, Inc..

Brose, David, and N'omi Greber (Eds.). (1979) *Hopewell Archaeology: The Chillicothe Conference.* Kent, OH: Kent State University Press.

Browman, David L. (1980) *Early Native Americans: Prehistoric Demography, Economy, and Technology.* New York: Mouton Publishers.

Brown, Ian W. (1981) *The Role of Salt in Eastern North American Prehistory.* Baton Rouge, LA: Louisiana Archaeological Survey and Antiquities Commission Anthropological Study, no. 3.

Brown, James A. (1975) *Perspectives in Cahokia Archaeology* (1975) Urbana, IL: Illinois Archaeological Survey, University of Illinois, Bulletin no. 10.

———. (1985) "The Mississippian Period," in Brose, Brown, and Penny, 1985: 93–146.

Bushnell, David Ives, Jr. (1904) *The Cahokia and Surrounding Mound Groups.* Cambridge, MA: Peabody Museum.

Cabeza de Vaca. (1907) *The Narrative of Álvar Núñez Cabeza de Vaca.* Trans. and ed. by Frederick W. Hodge, in Jameson: 1907.

———. (1961) *Adventures in the Unknown Interior of America.* Trans. by Cyclone Covey. New York: Collier Books.

Caddoan Mounds: Temples and Tombs of an Ancient People. (1984) Austin, TX: Texas Parks and Wildlife Department.

The Cahokia Mounds. (1929) Urbana, IL: University of Illinois.

Cahokia Brought to Life: An Artifactual Story of America's Great Monument. (1983 reprint) St. Louis, MO: The Greater St. Louis Archaeological Society.

Carlson, John B. (1979) "Hopewell: Prehistoric America's Golden Age," offprint from *Early Man* (Winter 1979). Chillicothe, OH: Craftsman Printing, Inc.

Ceram, C. W. [pseud. for Kurt W. Marek] (1971) *The First Americans.* New York: New American Library.

Champion, T. C. (Ed.). (1989) *Centre and Periphery: Comparative Studies in Archaeology.* London: Unwin Hyman.

Closs, Michael P. (1986) *Native American Mathematics.* Austin, TX: University of Texas.

Coe, Michael D., Dean Snow, and Elizabeth Benson. (1986) *Atlas of Ancient North America.* New York and Oxford: Facts on File Publications.

Cole, Fay Cooper. (1937) *Rediscovering Illinois, Archaeological Explorations in and around Fulton County.* Chicago: University of Chicago.

Covey, Cyclone (Trans. and Ed.). (1961) *Cabeza de Vaca's Adventures in the Unknown Interior of America.* New York: Collier Books.

Crosby, Alfred. (1972) *The Columbian Exchange: Biological and Cultural Consequences of 1492.* Westport, CT: Greenwood Press.

———. (1986) *Ecological Imperialism: The Biological Expansion of Europe, 900–1900.* Cambridge and New York: Cambridge University Press.

———. (1991) "Infectious Disease and Demography of the Atlantic Peoples," in *Journal of World History* 2 (2): 119–33.

Cutler, Hugh C., and Leonard W. Blake. (1969) "Corn from Cahokia Sites," in Fowler, 1969b: 122–36.

de Castaneda, Pedro. (1907) *The Narrative of the Expedition of Coronado.* Trans. and ed. by Frederick W. Hodge, in Jameson, 1907.

Denevan, William M. (Ed.). (1976) *The Native Populations of the Americas in 1492.* Madison: University of Wisconsin Press.

Deuel, Thorne. (1968 reprint) *American Indian Ways of Life: An Interpretation of the Archaeology of Illinois and Adjoining Regions.* (Orig. pub. 1958) Springfield, IL: Illinois State Museum, Story of Illinois, no. 9.

Dincauze, Dena F., and Robert J. Hasenstab. (1985) "Explaining the Iroquois: Tribalization on a Prehistoric Periphery," in Champion, 1989: 67–87.

Dobyns, Henry. (1983) *Their Number Become Thinned: Native American Population Dynamics in Eastern North America.* Knoxville: University of Tennesee.

Dragoo, Don W. (1963) *Mounds for the Dead: An Analysis of Adena Culture.* Pittsburgh: Carnegie Museum.

———. (1976) "Some Aspects of Eastern North American Prehistory: A Review 1975," in *American Antiquity*, 41 (1): 3–27.

Earle, T.K. (1989) "The Evolution of Chiefdoms," *Current Anthropology*, 30 (1): 84–88.

Early Man in America: Readings from Scientific American. (1973) San Francisco: W.H. Freeman and Company.

Eggan, Frederick R. (1952) "The Ethnological Cultures and Their Archaeological Backgrounds" in Griffin, 1952: 35–45.

Emerson, Thomas E. (1984) *The BBB Motor Site.* Urbana: University of Illinois Press.

———. (1982) *Mississippian Stone Images in Illinois.* Urbana: Illinois Archaeological Survey, Inc., University of Illinois at Urbana-Champagne, Circular no. 6.

———. (1988) "Water, Serpents, and the Underworld: An Exploration into Cahokian Symbolism," Manuscript.

Fagan, Brian M. (1991) *Ancient North America: The Archaeology of a Continent.* London and New York: Thames and Hudson.

Folsom, Franklin. (1971) *America's Ancient Treasures: Rand McNally Guide to U.S. Archaeological Sites and Museums.* Chicago: Rand McNally.

Ford, James Alfred, and Clarence Webb. (1956) *Poverty Point: A Late Archaic Site.* New York: Anthropological Papers of the American Museum of Natural History.

Ford, Richard I. (Ed.). (1978) *Early Food Production in North America.* Ann Arbor: University Museum of Anthropology, University of Michigan.

———. (1981) "Gardening and Farming before AD 1000: Patterns of Prehistoric Culture North of Mexico," *Journal of Ethnobiology* 1 (1): 6–7.

———. (Ed.). (1985) *Prehistoric Food Production in North America.* Ann Arbor: Museum of Anthropology, University of Michigan.

Fowler, Melvin L. (1969a) "The Cahokia Site," in Fowler, 1969b: 1–30.

———. (Ed.). (1969b) *Explorations into Cahokia Archaeology.* Urbana, IL: University of Illinois, Illinois Archaeological Survey, Bulletin no. 7.

———. (1974) *Cahokia: Ancient Capital of the Midwest.* Reading, MA: Addison-Wesley Publishing Co.

———. (1978) "Cahokia and the American Bottom: Settlement Archaeology," in Smith, 1978: 455–78.

———. (Ed.). (1975a) *Cahokia Archaeology: Field Reports.* Springfield, IL: Illinois State Museum Research Series: Papers in Anthropology, no. 3 (May).

———. (1975b) "A Pre-Columbian Urban Center on the Mississippi," in *Scientific American,* 233 (August).

Fowler, Melvin L., and R. L. Hall. (1975) "Archaeological Phases at Cahokia," in Brown, 1975: 1–14.

Fundaburk, Emma Lila, and Mary Douglass Fundaburk Foreman. (1981 reprint) *Sun Circles and Human Hands: The Southeastern Indians—Art and Industry.* (Original publication 1957) Fairhope, AL: Southern Publications.

Garcilaso de la Vega, the Inca. (1988) *The Florida of the Inca.* Trans. by John and Jeanette Varner. Austin, TX: University of Texas Press.

Gibson, Jon L. (1974) "Poverty Point, the First Native American Chiefdom," *Archaeology* 27 (2): 96–105.

———. (1980) "Speculations on the Origin and Development of Poverty Point Culture," in J. L. Gibson (Ed.), *Caddoan and Poverty Point Archaeology, Bulletin of the Louisiana Archaeological Society* 6: 321–48.

———. (1985) *Poverty Point: A Culture of the Lower Mississippi Valley.* 2nd Printing. Baton Rouge: Louisiana Archaeological Survey and Antiquities Commission, Anthropological Study no. 7.

Gilliland, Marion Spjut. (1975) *The Material Culture of Key Marco Florida.* Gainesville, FL: University Presses of Florida.

Goad, Sharon Iowa. (1978) "Exchange Networks in the Prehistoric Southeastern

United States," University of Georgia, Ph. D. Dissertation, University Micro-
films International no. 78–22, 311.

―――. (1979) "Middle Woodland Exchange in the Prehistoric Southeastern
United States," in Brose and Greber, 1979: 239–46.

―――. (1980) "Patterns of Late Archaic Exchange," in *Tennessee Archaeologist*, 5:1–16.

Goldstein, Lynne Gail. (1980) *Mississippi Mortuary Practices: A Case Study of
Two Cemetaries in the Lower Illinois Valley*. Evanston, IL: Northwestern University Archaeological Program, Scientific Papers, no. 4.

Goodman, Alan H., and George J. Armelagos. (1985) "Disease and Death at Dr.
Dickson's Mounds," *Natural History*, 94 (9): 12–18 (September).

Green, Michael D. (1982) *The Politics of Indian Removal: Creek Government and
Society in Crisis*. Lincoln and London: University of Nebraska Press.

Gregg, Michael L. (1975) "A Population Estimate for Cahokia," in Brown, 1975:
126–36.

Gregory, H.F. (Ed.) (1986) *The Southern Caddo: An Anthology*. New York: Gar-
land Publishing.

Griffin, James B. (Ed.) (1952) *The Archaeology of the Eastern United States*.
Chicago: University of Chicago Press.

―――. (1967) "Eastern North American Archaeology: A Summary," in *Science*,
156 (3772): 175–91 (14 April).

―――. (1979) "An Overview of the Chillicothe Hopewell Conference," in Brose
and Greber, 1979: 266–79.

―――. (1983) "The Midlands," in Jennings, 1983: 243–301.

Hall, Robert L. (1975) "Chronology and Phases at Cahokia," in Brown, 1975: 15–31.

―――. (1980) "An Interpretation of the Two-Climax Model of Illinois Prehistory," in Browman, 1980: 401–62.

Halley, David J. and James L. Rudolph. (1986) *Mississippi Period Archaeology of
the Georgia Piedmont*. Athens, GA: University of Georgia Laboratory of Archaeology Series, Report no. 24, Georgia Archaeological Research Design
Papers, no. 2.

Hamilton, Henry W., Jean Tyree Hamilton, and Eleanor F. Chapman. (1974)
Spiro Mound Copper. Columbia, MO: *Memoir Missouri Archaeological Society*, no. 11.

Hasenstab, Robert J. (1984) "A Core-Periphery Model for Mississippian-Iroquoian
Interaction during the Late Prehistoric Period in North America." Manuscript.

Headrick, Daniel R. (1981) *Tools of Empire: Technology and European Imperialism in the 19th Century*. New York and Oxford: Oxford University Press.

Helms, Mary W. (1975) *Middle America: A Culture History of Heartland and
Frontiers*. Englewood Cliffs, NJ: Prentice Hall.

Hodge, Frederick W. (Trans. and Ed.). (1907) *The Narrative of Álvar Núñez
Cabeza de Vaca*, in Jameson, 1907.

Howard, James H. (1968) *The Southeastern Ceremonial Complex and Its Interpretation*. Columbia, MO: *Memoir Missouri Archaeological Society*, no. 6.

Hudson, Charles M. (1976) *The Southeastern Indians*. Knoxville: University of
Tennesee Press.

Hyde, George E. (1962) *Indians of the Woodlands: From Prehistoric Times to
1725*. Norman, OK: University of Oklahoma Press.

Iseminger, William R. (1980) "Cahokia: A Mississippi Metropolis," in *Historic Illinois*, Vol. 2, no. 6 (April) 1–4.
———. (1980) "Yes, A True Metropolis," *Cahokian*, reprinted in Norrish, 1983: 12–13.
———. (1986) "Excavations at Cahokia Mounds," in *Archaeology* (January/February 1986) 58–59.
Jameson, J. Franklin (Ed.). (1907) *Original Narratives of Early American History: Spanish Explorers in the Southern United States, 1528–1543*. New York: Charles Scribner's Sons. Includes: Frederick W. Hodge (Trans. and Ed.), *The Narrative of Álvar Núñez Cabeza de Vaca*; Theodore H. Lewis (Trans. and Ed.), *The Narrative of the Expedition of Hernando de Soto by the Gentleman of Elvas*; and Frederick W. Hodge (Trans. and Ed.), *The Narrative of the Expedition of Coronado, by Pedro de Castaneda.*
Jane, Cecil (Ed.). (1988) *The Four Voyages of Columbus*. New York: Dover Publications.
Jennings, Francis. (1976) *The Invasion of America: Indians, Colonialism, and the Cant of Conquest*. New York: W. W. Norton.
Jennings, Jesse D. (1983) *Ancient Native Americans*. 2nd Edition. San Francisco: W. H. Freeman.
———. (1989) *Prehistory of North America*. 3rd Edition. Mountain View, CA: Mayfield Publishing Company.
Johnson, Alfred E. (1979) "Kansas City Hopewell," in Brose and Greber, 1979: 86–93.
Keegan, William F. (1987) *The Emergent Horticultural Economies of the Eastern Woodlands*. Carbondale, IL: Southern Illinois University, Center for Archaeological Investigations, Occasional Paper 7.
Klein, Barry T. (Ed.). (1990) *Reference Encyclopedia of the American Indian*, 5th Edition. West Nyack, NY: Todd Publications.
Kopper, Philip. (1986) *The Smithsonian Book of North American Indians Before the Coming of the Europeans*. Washington, D.C.: Smithsonian Books.
Krupp, E.C. (1977) "Cahokia: Corn, Commerce, and the Cosmos," *Griffith Observer*, 41 (5) (May): 10–20.
Lallo, John, Jerome Carl Rose, and George J. Armelagos (1980), "An Ecological Interpretation of Variation in Mortality within Three Prehistoric American Indian Populations from Dickson Mounds," in Browman, 1980: 203–38.
Larson, Lewis H. Jr. (1972) "Functional Considerations of Warfare in the Southeast during the Mississippi Period," in *American Antiquity* 37 (3): 383–92.
Lathrap, Donald W. (1977) "Our Father the Cayman, Our Mother the Gourd: Spinden Revisited, or A Unitary Model for the Emergence of Agriculture in the New World," in Charles A. Reed, *Origins of Agriculture* (The Hague: Mouton, 1977).
———. (1987) "The Introduction of Maize in Prehistoric Eastern North America: The View from Amazonia and the Santa Elena Peninsula," in Keegan, 1987: 345–71.
Lee, Susan. (1992) "The Hunchback Effigy Ceramics of the Prehistoric Southeast." Thesis in progress, University of Arkansas, Department of Anthropology, Fayetteville.
Lewis, R. Barry. (1982) *Two Mississippian Hamlets in the Cairo Lowland of*

Southeast Missouri. Urbana, IL: Illinois Archaeological Survey, Special Publication no. 2.

Lewis, Theodore H. (Trans. and Ed.). (1907) *The Narrative of the Expedition of Hernando DeSoto by the Gentleman of Elvas,* in Jameson: 1907.

Mahon, John K. (1988) "Indian-United States Military Situation, 1775–1848," in Washburn, 1988: 144–62.

McNeill, William H. (1976) *Plagues and Peoples.* Garden City, NY: Doubleday Anchor Books.

Meggers, Betty J. (1972) *Prehistoric America.* Chicago: Aldine Publishing Co.

Milanich, Jerald T., and Charles H. Fairbanks. (1980) *Florida Archaeology.* New York: Academic Press.

Milanich, Jerald, and Samuel Proctor. (1978) *Tacachale: Essays on the Indians of Florida and Southeastern Georgia during the Historic Period.* Gainesville, FL: University Presses of Florida.

Mills, William Corless. (1926) *Certain Mounds and Village Sites in Ohio.* Columbus, OH: Press of F. J. Heer.

Milner, George R. (1983) *The East St. Louis Stone Quarry Site Cemetary* (11-S–468). Urbana, IL: University of Illinois.

Mohrman, Harold, and Dick Norrish. (n.d.) *The Cahokia Mounds: A Guidebook.* Collinsville, IL: Cahokia Mounds Museum Society.

Mooney, James. (1894) "The Siouan Tribes of the East," Bureau of American Ethnology, Bulletin V (22): 1–101.

Moorehead, Warren K., Jay L.B. Taylor, Morris M. Leighton, and Frank C. Baker. (1929) *The Cahokia Mounds.* Urbana: University of Illinois.

Morgan, William N. (1980) *Prehistoric Architecture in the Eastern United States.* Cambridge, MA: Massachusetts Institute of Technology Press.

Morse, Dan F., and Phyllis A. Morse. (1982) *Archaeology of the Central Mississippi Valley.* New York: Academic Press (HBJ).

Nash, Gary B. (1982) *Red, White, and Black: The Peoples of Early America,* 2nd Edition. Englewood Cliffs, NJ: Prentice-Hall.

Nassaney, Michael S. (1989) "Spatial-Temporal Dimensions of Social Integration During the Coles Creek Period in Central Arkansas." Amherst: University of Massachusetts, Dept. of Anthropology. Paper.

Nassaney, Michael S., and C. R. Cobb (Eds.). *Late Woodland Stability, Transformation, and Variation in the Greater Southeast.* Manuscript.

National Resources Committee [U.S. Government]. (1937) *Drainage Basin Problems and Programs—December 1936.* Washington: U.S. Government Printing Office.

Neuman, Robert W. (1984) *An Introduction to Louisiana Archaeology.* Baton Rouge: Louisiana State University Press.

Neuman, Robert W., and Nancy W. Hawkins. (1987) *Louisiana Prehistory.* Baton Rouge, LA: Louisiana Archaeological Survey and Antiquities Commission, Anthropological Study no. 6 (April).

Norrish, Dick. (1975) "Horseshoe Lake: A Supply Center," *Cahokian* (September 1975) reprinted in Norrish, 1983: 36–38.

———. (1978) "Woodhenge—Work of a Genius," *Cahokian* reprinted in Norrish, 1983: 17–27.

———. (1980a) "A True Metropolis? Interview with James W. Porter," *Cahok-*

ian reprinted in Norrish, 1983: 12–13.

————. (1980b) "World Honor Is Official," *Cahokian* reprinted in Norrish, 1983: 49–50.

———— (Ed.). (1983) *Best of Cahokian: 16 Articles Appearing in the Cahokian, 1974–1980.* Revised Edition, with 19 Articles, 1974–1983. Collinsville, IL: Cahokia Mounds Museum Society.

————. (1969) "Some Ceramic Periods and Their Implications at Cahokia," in Fowler, 1969b: 100–22.

O'Brien, Patricia J. (1972) *A Formal Analysis of Cahokia Ceramics from the Powell Tract.* Urbana, IL: Illinois Archaeological Survey, Monograph no. 3.

————. (1972) "Urbanism, Cahokia and Middle Mississippian," *Archaeology*, 25 (3): 189–97 (June).

O'Donnell, James Howlett III. (1982) *Southeastern Frontiers: Europeans, Africans, and American Indians, 1513–1840.* Bloomington, IN: Indiana University Press.

Parmalee, Paul W. (1975) "A General Summary of the Vertebrate Fauna from Cahokia," in Brown, 1975: 137–55.

Penny, David W. (1985). "The Late Archaic Period," in Brose, Brown, and Penny, 1985: 15–42.

Penny, James S. (1986) *The Prehistoric Peoples of Southern Illinois.* Carbondale: Center for Archaeological Investigations, Southern Illinois University at Carbondale.

Pfeiffer, John E. (1974) *Indian City on the Mississippi,* Offprint from *Time-Life Nature/Science Annual.* Collinsville, IL: Cahokia Mounds Museum Society.

Porter, James Warren. (1969) "The Mitchell Site and Prehistoric Exchange Systems at Cahokia: AD 1000 +/–300," in Fowler, 1969b: 137–64.

Powell, Mary Lucas. (1988) *Status and Health in Prehistory: A Case Study of the Moundville Chiefdom.* Washington D.C.: Smithsonian Institution Press.

Prufer, Olaf H. (1964) "The Hopewell Cult," *Scientific American,* 211 (6).

Ramenovsky, Ann. (1987) *Vectors of Death: The Archaeology of European Contact.* Albuquerque: University of New Mexico Press.

Reed, Nelson A. (1969) "Monks' and Other Mississippian Mounds," in Fowler, 1969b: 31–42.

Rowe, Chandler W. (1956) *The Effigy Mound Culture of Wisconsin.* Milwaukee, WI: Milwaukee Public Museum, Publications in Anthropology no. 3.

Russell, Howard S. (1980) *Indian New England Before the Mayflower.* Hanover, NH: University Press of New England.

Seeman, Mark F. (1979) "Feasting with the Dead: Ohio Hopewell Charnel House Ritual as a Context for Redistribution," in Brose and Greber, 1979: 39–46.

Silverberg, Robert. (1986) *Mound Builders of Ancient America: The Archaeology of a Myth.* (Orig. pub. 1968.) Athens, OH: Ohio University Press.

Smith, Bruce D. (Ed.). (1978) *Mississippian Settlement Patterns.* New York: Academic Press.

————. (1986) "The Archaeology of the Southeastern United States: From Dalton to de Soto, 10,500–500 B.P.," in Wendorf and Close, 1986: 1–92.

————. (1987) "The Independent Domestication of Indigenous Seed-Bearing Plants in Eastern North America," in Keegan, 1987: 3–48.

————. (Ed.). (1990) *Mississippian Emergence: The Evolution of Agricultural*

Societies in the Eastern Woodlands. Washington, D.C.: Smithsonian Press.

Smith, Harriet M. (1969) "The Murdock Mound: Cahokia Site," in Fowler, 1969b: 49–88.

Squier, Ephraim G., and Edwin H. Davis. (1973 reprint) *Ancient Monuments of the Mississippi Valley.* (Orig. pub. 1848) New York: AMS Press for Harvard Peabody Museum.

Stoltman, James B. (1966) "New Radiocarbon Dates for Southeastern Fiber-Tempered Pottery," in *American Antiquity* 31 (6): 872–74.

Streuver, Stuart, and Felicia Antonelli Holton. (1979) *Koster: Americans in Search of Their Prehistoric Past.* New York: Doubleday & Co. Signet Book.

Strong, John W. (1978) "Tracking the Maya Connection," *Cahokian* reprinted in Norrish, 1983: 39.

———. (1979–80) "Birdman: the Search for Meaning I, II, and III," *Cahokian* (July 1979; February 1980; July 1980), reprinted in Norrish, 1983: 40–48.

Stuart, George E. (1972) "Who Were the Mound Builders?" *National Geographic* 142 (6): 782–801 (December).

Sturtevant, William C. (Ed.). (1979–) *Handbook of North American Indians.* Washington, D.C.: Smithsonian Institution Press.

Swanton, John R. (1911) *Indian Tribes of the Lower Mississippi Valley and Adjacent Coast of the Gulf of Mexico.* Washington, D.C.: Smithsonian Institute, Bureau of American Ethnology, Bulletin 43.

Tesser, Carmen Chaves, and Charles Hudson. (1991) "Before Oglethorpe: Hispanic and Indian Cultures in the Southeast United States," in *Magazine of History* Columbian Quincentenary Issue, 5 (4): 43–46 (Spring).

Thomas, Cyrus. (1985 reprint) *Report on the Mound Explorations of the Bureau of Ethnology.* (Orig. pub. 1894) Washington, D.C.: Smithsonian Institution Press.

Thornton, Russell. (1987) *American Indian Holocaust and Survival: A Population History since 1492.* Norman, OK: University of Oklahoma.

Tooker, Elizabeth. (1971) "Clans and Moieties in North America," *Current Anthropology* 12 (3): 357–76 (June).

Trail Guide: Poverty Point State Commemorative Area. (n.p.; n.d.).

Varner, John Grier, and Jeanette Johnson Varner (Trans. and Eds.). (1988) *The Florida of the Inca* by Garcilaso de la Vega, the Inca. Austin, TX: University of Texas Press.

Vidal-Naquet, Pierre (Ed.). (1987) *Harper Atlas of World History.* (English trans. of *Le Grand Livre de l'histoire du monde,* Paris: Hachette, 1986) New York: Harper and Row.

Vogel, Joseph O. (1975) "Trends in Cahokia Ceramics: Preliminary Study of the Collections from Tracts 15A and 15B," in Brown, 1975: 32–125.

Walthall, John A. (1977) *Moundville: An Introduction to the Archaeology of a Mississippian Chiefdom.* University, AL: University of Alabama, Alabama Museum of Natural History.

———. (1979) "Hopewell and the Southern Heartland," in Brose and Greber, 1979: 200–208.

———. (1981) *Galena and Aboriginal Trade in Eastern North America,* Springfield, IL: Illinois State Museum, Scientific Papers, Vol XVII.

Webb, Clarence H. (1959) *The Belcher Mound.* Salt Lake City: Society for American Archaeology.

————. (1982) *The Poverty Point Culture*. Baton Rouge: Louisiana State University, Museum of Geoscience.

Wendorf, F., and A.D. Close (Eds.). (1986) *Advances in World Archaeology*. Vol. 5. New York: Academic Press.

Will, George F., and George E. Hyde. (1964 Reprint) *Corn Among the Indians of the Upper Missouri*. (Orig. pub. 1917). Lincoln, NE: University of Nebraska.

Williamson, Ray A. (1984) *Living the Sky: The Cosmos of the American Indian*. Boston: Houghton-Mifflin.

Wilson, Terry P. (1988) *The Osage*. New York and Philadelphia: Chelsea House Publishers.

Wittry, Warren L. (1969) "The American Woodhenge," in Fowler, 1969b: 43–48.

Wray, Donald. "The Archaeology of the Illinois Valley: 1950," in Griffin, 1952.

Zubrow, Ezra B.W., Margaret C. Fritz, and John M. Fritz (Eds.). (1974) *New World Archaeology: Theoretical and Cultural Transformations; Readings from Scientific American*. San Francisco: W.H. Freeman and Company.

INDEX

Lynda Norene Shaffer did her undergraduate work at the University of Texas and received a Ph.D. in East Asian and American history from Columbia University. A founding member of the World History Association, she has served three terms on its National Council. She is currently a member of the Tufts University History Department. Both her scholarly and teaching interests include China, Native Americans, and world history.